THE AGENTIC BANK

RE-ENGINEERING FINANCE BEYOND HUMAN LIMITS

JOHN BLICQ AND TIM TOHOLKA

DISCLAIMER

The Agentic Bank – Re-Engineering Finance Beyond Human Limits

First Edition

ISBN paperback: 978-1-7643691-0-7
ISBN ebook: 978-1-7643691-1-4

The information, opinions, and recommendations contained in this book are provided for general guidance only and do not constitute professional advice. While every effort has been made to ensure accuracy and relevance, readers should consult qualified experts for advice tailored to their specific circumstances. The authors and publishers do not accept any liability for actions taken based on this content. All examples and scenarios are illustrative and may not reflect actual outcomes in your organisation or industry. The authors used fictional company and individual names; any resemblance to real entities would be coincidental.

Published by:

Innovations Accelerated

TABLE OF CONTENTS

FOREWORDS – Who is this book for? Why this book and why now?

Throughout history, major shifts—like the move from steam to electricity in the Industrial Revolution—have redefined how work is structured. Today, Agentic AI is driving a similar transformation. Unlike traditional automation, Agentic AI can perceive, decide, and adapt independently. This technology isn't just an extension of human labour; it's a separate cognitive force poised to create self-optimizing organizations. The change ahead is not incremental but foundational, requiring companies to build around AI agents as core units of work and value.

This book was written for the decision-makers who sense the ground shifting under their feet.

Who this book is for?

If you are a leader inside a bank, insurer, or wealth-management firm — or an investor, policymaker, technologist, or advisor who shapes the destiny of those institutions — this book was written with you squarely in mind. It assumes you already understand the materiality of digital transformation and have wrestled with open banking, cloud migration, and ever-faster payment rails. What you hold now is the next set of questions:

- How do we move beyond "AI pilots" to an organisation that runs on agentic intelligence?
- How do we protect trust and brand equity when products commoditise and experiences become the only differentiator?

- How do we re-skill thousands of knowledge workers when tasks they have mastered for decades can now be delegated to software agents?

Whether you sit in a C-suite, on a board, in a strategy or innovation function, or lead a product tribe charged with "the next big thing," this book serves as a field manual. It equips you to translate hype into road-mapped capability, regulatory compliance, and commercial value.

How to read this book?

The book follows a consistent structure for ease and speed of read. Like you the authors are busy executives needing to go to the essence of the information and then do their best to apply it in their business context.

You will find:

- A short intro to each chapter

- An opening vignette or real-world use case designed to set the scene for the reader.

- Articulation of the components of the chapters designed to bring you to the essence of the matter.

- A "So What" designed to help you relate to the matter.

- A C-Suite check list to help you with a guideline on what you should be on the look for to implement Agentic AI within your organization.

- Finally, a "Key Take-Away" section.

If you are in a hurry, we recommend you focus on the So What, C-Suite checklist and Key Take-Aways.

Being realistic, the reader needs to bear in mind that this book will be obsolete very soon. What will remain is the thinking framework that this book is designed to help the reader identify and hopefully integrate.

The authors made a particular effort in adding up to date external resources and references supporting the narrative. We highly encourage the reader to explore these references as they provide deeper understanding on Agentic AI and its immediate adjacencies.

The authors, throughout the book, embedded quotes and citations which are fictional and for illustrative purposes only. It is explicitly mentioned, and its only purpose is to provide concrete examples of the transformation potential of Agentic AI in Financial Services.

Why this book?

We (the authors) have spent the past decade helping financial institutions absorb wave after wave of technological change — mobile, APIs, cloud, data science, blockchain, and the first generation of generative AI and digital twins. Each wave promised reinvention; most delivered only incremental improvement.

Agentic AI is different. It does not merely *assist* employees; it *acts on behalf of customers and institutions* with autonomy, memory, and a growing toolset. The shift is not from clerks to chat-bots but from *interfaces* to *digital colleagues* you can delegate to. That step function forces a re-architecting of operating models, risk frameworks, and the very meaning of "customer relationship."

Yet, when we look across the industry, we see two camps:

Camp	Symptom	Risk
Cautious observers	Wait-and-see stance, short Proof of Concepts (POCs), no budget for governance	They arrive late and discover moats have moved to data, not balance-sheet scale
Speed racers	"Deploy GPT" edicts, patchwork of point solutions	They create fragmented agent colonies and unmanageable systemic risk

Both camps need a structured guide that blends strategy, technology, regulation, and human-centred design. That is why this book exists. It distils the lessons, patterns, and frameworks we have developed in boardrooms, codebases, and regulatory sandboxes around the world into a single, actionable narrative.

Why now?

Timing matters. As this foreword goes to print (late-2025), three forces are converging:

1. Maturing agent frameworks – Open-source stacks such as AutoGen and CrewAI, plus vendor suites from major cloud providers, have lowered the build/buy barrier dramatically. A functional agentic prototype can be stood up in weeks, not quarters.

2. Regulatory clarity – The EU AI Act, Australia's Safe AI Framework, and parallel efforts in the US and Singapore have turned "wait for the rules" into "comply or concede." The contours of lawful, responsible autonomy are now visible.

3. Customer acclimatisation, Voice-activated mortgage switches, auto-invest rebalancers, parametric insurance payouts: these are no longer demos. Main-street consumers have tasted what friction-free, context-aware finance feels like, and their tolerance for laggards is plummeting.

History tells us that when technological capability, regulatory permission, and consumer expectation align, industries are reshaped at pace. The window for deliberate, well-planned adoption is *open but narrowing*.

In the next 18–24 months, the winners will be those who:

- Build data-native ecosystems so agents operate on trusted, real-time context.
- Architect for governed autonomy, embedding auditability and ethics by design.
- Obsess over experience networks, recognising that brand loyalty now sits at the intersection of relevance, convenience, and trust.

This book provides the scaffolding to do exactly that. It maps the terrain, dives into sector-specific value plays, lays out the execution muscle, and helps you future-proof against the next discontinuity. It will also provide you with a view of the future which will highlight how unprepared your organisation is to deal with the disruption. This chapter is designed to spark conversation within your organisation and hopefully get you started to mitigate the strategic risks.

Read it cover to cover or jump straight to the chapters that address your most urgent questions. Either way, use it as a working document: annotate the margins, challenge the assumptions, and translate the frameworks into your own playbooks.

The age of the Agentic Bank is not a thought experiment; it is an unfolding competitive reality. The institutions that act with clarity and courage now will define the next decade of financial services. The rest will look back on this moment as a missed fork in the strategic road.

Welcome to the fork.

INTRODUCTION – The Rise of Agentic AI in Financial Services

When we published *Metaverse & Financial Services* (2022) the headline was **presence**: virtual worlds, digital identities and phygital assets redefining where and how value is exchanged. Three short years later the headline has shifted from presence to **agency**—the power to act. Large-language models, multi-modal transformers and neuro-symbolic systems have collided with cloud economics, real-time payments, and decentralized ledgers. The result is a financial stack that no longer waits for people to push buttons; it anticipates, adapts and—crucially—**bargains**.

Before diving deep into the topic, the reader must take a step back and reflect as to why strategic design, strategic thinking and innovation matters.

Why long-term thinking and innovation matters

A common experience for the innovation community, is to have their work, described by senior executives as "utopic".

They are right because in a corporate world the reality is bounded by profit and losses, assets and liabilities, and time is counted on a 12-month horizon divided in weeks, months, quarters, semesters, and financial year.

Increased visibility and scrutiny from Boards, with increased personal accountability to protect the company and its stakeholders (investors, people, regulators, community), mean management have an increased focus on value generation.

Even if they think on a multiyear horizon, senior executives' reality is grounded and timebound to deliver short-term outcomes. It is the Board responsibility to influence management to prepare their organisation for beyond the near term to build a sustainable future.

Innovators and strategists have a duty to work on a different time horizon. They must see the world with different lenses; they must pick up signals of emerging trends which will impact the value chain of the company they serve.

For an innovator or a strategist, thinking 12 months (short term) is simply not possible. It would anchor the thinking in the finite game where competitors remain the same. Where customers, society and collective consciousness are static. A 12-month world doesn't change and there is little to learn about, nothing to adapt to.

Instead, innovators and strategists project their thinking in long-term horizons or the infinite game. Once you break free from the constraints of a static environment endless possibilities emerge. The work of the innovators is to identify and make sense of the trends which will impact the future of their organisation.

The theory highlighted in this book would not be possible in 12-month anchored thinking. We will see that digital twins will likely become multi-generational digital assets. We will see that the Metaverse can create entire new industries and revolutionise existing ones.

As innovators, our work can be described as utopic but here are some examples of utopia which have changed the world we live in and left well-established incumbents into business school cases of failure to adapt:

- The utopia of a spherical Earth (Copernicus 1543) challenging the almighty Catholic Church dogma and opening the minds for scientific exploration. (We can confidently say that Copernicus was right too early. It's saddening to witness that, despite undeniable scientific evidence; 500 years later some people are still convinced that Earth is flat.)

- The utopia of spreading knowledge across the world. Leading to the invention of the printing machine (Gutenberg 1439).

- The utopia of finding a shorter and quicker route to the Indies (Christopher Columbus 1492) leading to the discovery of a vast new continent and unknown advanced civilisations.

- The utopia of the enlightenment offering mind space for a world in which people would be free to choose their beliefs and experience different forms of governance than total monarchy. This led the people of France to their Revolution, opening a pathway to modern democracies.

- Closer to our time, the utopia of sending people into space and to the Moon; propelling research and science leading to life changing discoveries and pushing the boundaries of our earthly reality. At the time of writing this book, NASA had landed its rover "Perseverance" on Mars with the mission to find traces of former life on the red planet.

These few examples demonstrate why utopia matters and how it can change the world. Let us have a quick look at what was utopia only a decade ago is now changing the reality of the financial services value chain.

Thought experiment – tomorrow's world.

It is the morning of July 14, 2035, at 6.30 am your smart implant (they have replaced smartphones about 5 years ago) gently buzzes your cerebrum (the part of the brain that controls senses) to wake you from a restful night. An electric signal is induced and makes your eardrums hear a pleasant nature soundscape. After 5 minutes of this music, you slowly bring your consciousness back to your body. You get out of bed and your preferred selected information is projected onto your optic nerves. You received a message from a relative living across the world, the weather will be great, and you have an appointment with your digital doctor at 1 pm.

You also have 126 meetings today, all taking place on the Metaverse. Your attendance is required at three of them. Your intellectual property licence renewal with your main client at 10 am; your IP lawyer at 12 pm to seal the new contract and; your Agentic banker at 3 pm. Be ready for this one as you are likely to get a new home loan by leveraging the financial performance of your enhanced AI powered digital twin. You have trained it for months with new IP downloads to generate 15.7% more income with your targeted audience. You will be handling your negotiation with your client's counterpart and their bot lawyer. It is an important conversation, but your results have been outstanding, your IP has delivered output that ranked in the top 5% of their digital employees. No need to worry. Your digital twin will be your wingman. It will handle the conversation with the bot lawyer and lead the client presentation on a different channel. In fact, the contractual key terms have already been pre-agreed two years ago and your compliance in meeting the service level agreement is recorded on your private blockchain.

You get in the shower for a fresh start. Meanwhile you ask your digital twin for an update of the work achieved last night. There were 36 transactions for a total of $2,568 — 70% with other digital twins, 27% with digital humans and 3% with humans. Not bad for a restful night. Interestingly you note that your digital twin has increased transactions with Digital Humans located in France by 7.33% over the past three days. Perhaps you should reinforce your agentic presence in French speaking countries. You ask your digital twin to ensure it has updated all its knowledge modules in French. You also ask him to increase marketing expenses on your French professional holographic demo.

Now that you are refreshed, it is time for your morning walk on the beach with the family. Don't forget to put sunscreen on, UVs are high today and, don't be late for your human meeting in three hours.

Science fiction or reality?

What I describe sounds like science fiction but the likelihood of this scenario arising may surprise you. William Gibson is often quoted in the innovation community, he said "The future is already here, it's simply not evenly distributed".

All the necessary external conditions (NECs) exist for this scenario to occur. To the best of my knowledge, they are just not yet connected.

Will this raise many philosophical, ethical, medical, legal questions? Of course, it will, but it's not the first time that our species enhances itself. Wearing prescription glasses, hearing devices, replacing a broken tooth, having a pacemaker implanted, using a prosthesis to replace a lost limb, undertaking surgery to have an artificial heart implanted are all forms of human enhancement.

In late 2020, the European Union (EU) approved the launch to market for artificial hearts from the French company Carmat[1]. In 2025, Elon Musk's Neuralink[2], implanted its brain chip in five human patients. Early trials have demonstrated that individuals with paralysis can control computers using only their thoughts. All the previous examples are forms of bionic humans. Our generation does not even consider

1 https://innovationorigins.com/green-light-for-european-artificial-heart/

2 https://www.businessinsider.com/als-neuralink-patient-edits-video-brain-ai-voice-elon-musk-2025-5

this enhancement bionic due to their commonality. Imagine the reaction of our grandparents or great grandparents if we could have told them their wounds and permanent injuries from experiencing two world wars could be mended with this sort of technology. They would probably consider it impossible. Our grandchildren or great grandchildren are likely to have the same feeling about us when it comes to the metaverse and digital twins.

Some core components of the thought experiment we went through earlier in this book are already available, it's a matter of time for these technologies to scale and reach the masses. We are going to go through it in detail.

But first and foremost, here are some reasons why this metaverse – agentic AI - digital twin scenario could well apply to a significant portion of the developed world.

The western world, at the turn of the early 90s made a strategic decision to transform their economies from being heavily driven by manufacturing to becoming more oriented toward services. The environment was very favourable for that shift, well-educated population, higher level of potential growth for the services industry, rising manufacturing capability and cheap labour from "Asian tigers" (China, Taiwan, South Korea, Vietnam).

We have reached a point where modern western economies rely on services for more than 70% of their GDP. According to the European Central Bank, the percentage of GDP driven by the services industry, in 2023, was 73.1% for the [3]EU and 80.5% for the US. In service-oriented economies, workers no longer deliver physical and tangible outcomes in the form of products. Rather, workers monetise their knowledge, and experience to their employers. It is a form of exclusive intellectual

3 https://www.ecb.europa.eu/mopo/eaec/html/index.en.html

property licencing. Each worker is unique, and their work is the result of their identity such as personal (values, beliefs, education) and professional qualifications and experience.

For a significant period between the 1990s and the mid-2000s, collaborative technologies were not sufficiently advanced to enable remote working at scale.

In the current context, accelerated by a global pandemic of COVID-19, the professional world has had no choice but to embrace remote working, collaborative tools and, more importantly, digital transformation. Early 2022, Bill Gates did predict that by 2025, most meetings will take place on the Metaverse. At time of writing, (May 2025) this prediction has proven dramatically wrong; however, it is probably accurate that most meetings are taking place on platforms like Microsoft Teams, Zoom or Google Meet. Although timing is inaccurate, the vision is probably correct as this space is fast evolving.

Although we are witnessing a trend of "return to work", even in tech companies, remote working is likely to remain embedded into our habits and perhaps it will even become the norm. Should this materialise, it will reshape urban dynamics. But more importantly, it will force rethinking the notion of location and productivity. This represents a shift in management style requirements. If physical presence was associated with control and productivity, COVID-19 probably challenges that paradigm.

As we transitioned overnight from the routine of commuting and clocking in/out to full remote working and lockdowns, we discovered a new form of work/freedom addiction.

In terms of the benefits, workers have saved a significant amount of time in avoiding the commute to work and enjoyed more personal disposable times.

But on the downside, workers have experienced an invasion of their private space (home) by work. This physical amalgamation and urging need to be connected has driven people to work extended hours. This has likely led to a surge of productivity for their employers. According to a Boston Consulting Group[4] survey of 12,000 professionals in various countries, 75% of employees said that during the first few months of the pandemic they have been able to maintain or improve productivity on their individual tasks.

It is difficult to now consider a return to the previous world. A hybrid model of mixed remote and onsite working is likely to prevail, but a scenario of full remote working isn't to discard neither for some industries.

This book talks largely about Agentic AI as a key component the next human evolution which is being augmented by technology.

Now that we have painted a complex (and partial) view of the trends shaping the future of our world, let's try to decomplexify the significant AI revolution underway.

4 https://www.bcg.com/en-au/publications/2020/valuable-productivity-gains-covid-19

CHAPTER 1 – A Quiet Revolution: Why Agentic AI Now?

In a near future, business review headline will read: *(the following statement is purely illustrative, and the person and Bank cited are fictional)*

"Our agents settled the FX hedge, flagged a liquidity gap, and drafted a board update—all before the first espresso finished pouring." —
Mei-Ling Chen, CFO, Pacific Horizon Bank

Financial-services leaders like Chen aren't talking about a distant future. Over the last 18 months her mid-tier Asian bank rewired hundreds of routine decisions—credit limits, margin calls, customer outreach—so they are now *made* by autonomous software colleagues. The P&L impact is real: a four-point cost-to-income improvement, 180 basis points of capital liberated, and happier regulators who can replay every agent decision in seconds.

If you run a bank, insurer, or wealth platform today, you already feel the same pressure: faster client expectations, thinner margins, and a regulatory drumbeat that demands explainable, resilient AI—*yesterday*. This chapter sets the stage. We'll decode what "agentic AI" really is, why the clock is ticking for financial firms, and how early movers are already separating from the pack.

Opening Vignette – The Six-Minute Wake-Up Call

In today's hyper-connected markets, every second counts—and nowhere is that more apparent than in Chen's Monday morning ritual. Before most of us have even poured our first coffee, a trio of autonomous agents has already scanned global markets, executed complex

FX strategies, and prepared an executive-ready briefing. What unfolds in those six crisp minutes isn't science fiction; it's the new heartbeat of finance, where precision-governed AI works seamlessly alongside human judgment to turn volatility into opportunity—no extra keystrokes required.

This opening vignette doesn't just illustrate speed; it embodies a paradigm shift. It's a wake-up call that autonomous systems, when tightly governed, can perform at scales and speeds far beyond any trading floor of the past. As we explore the mechanics and governance of agent-driven finance, remember: those six minutes aren't magic—they're the future of decision-making in motion.

Monday 08:59, Singapore. Equity futures spike, the yen jumps. An internal alert pings Chen's phone: *JPY-USD volatility 2σ above trend; hedge expiring in 11 min.*

09:00—An FX-hedging agent scrapes live market depth, models ten hedge paths, and proposes three. Chen taps *"Approve Path 2"* in the mobile dashboard.

09:05—Trades execute across three liquidity venues, collateral is released, ledger entries post. A second agent sweeps surplus yen into a money-market fund to earn 28 hours of extra yield until payroll hits.

09:06—Board summary auto-draft pops up for review: *"Closed hedge #772; avoided potential MTM loss US$1.7 m; ROE +8 bps."*

Six minutes, three agents, zero human keystrokes. Not magic—just tightly-governed autonomy.

From Chatty to Agentic Large language models (LLMs)

LLMs grabbed headlines for writing essays and code on cue. Useful—but still waiting for *us* to decide what matters. **Agentic AI goes a step further:** it senses context, sets its own micro-goals, chooses tools, and acts. Think of an analyst who not only drafts the memo but also attaches the reconciled numbers, sends it to the right approver, and books the resulting trade once signed-off.

Spot the Difference

	Generative AI	**Agentic AI**
Trigger	Human prompt	Event, schedule, or drift in KPI
Output	Text, code, images	Real-world state change (booking, payment, risk limit)
Memory	Ephemeral context	Long-term vector + graph store
Tools	None or single API	Chained tools: pricing, payments, CRM, risk engine
Governance	Prompt hygiene	Policy engine + audit ledger

Put simply, generative AI *creates content*; agentic AI *creates outcomes*—with an audit trail regulator can trace.

1.2 Why Finance Can't Wait

Here are a few illustrations highlighting the urgency for financial services organisation to understand Agentic AI.

1. **Margin compression meets instant expectations.** Customers are trained by food-delivery apps. They now ask: *why does a mortgage still take a week?* Agents condense "time-to-yes" to minutes, capturing wallet share before rivals even quote.

2. **Regulators codify accountability.** The EU AI Act[5], APRA CPS 230[6], MAS AI[7] guidelines, OCC bulletins, and NIST AI-RMF converge on one theme: *explain, monitor, and control your AI.* Agentic architectures with policy-as-code tick those boxes early turning compliance from drag to moat.

3. **Capital flows faster than IT change cycles.** Agent-native fintechs can pivot overnight. Incumbents must shrink the idea-to-impact cycle or bleed profitable niches. Bain estimates that by 2027, 25 percent of retail-bank revenue growth will accrue to firms running "autonomous product factories."

4. **Talent gravitates to empowerment.** The best quants and product managers want to *ship* ideas, not file Jira tickets for IT queues. Firms that hand them an agent framework win the talent war.

---

5 https://eur-lex.europa.eu/legal-content/EN/TXT/?uri=CELEX:52021PC0206

6 https://www.apra.gov.au/operational-risk-management

7 https://www.mas.gov.sg/-/media/mas-media-library/publications/monographs-or-information-paper/imd/2024/information-paper-on-ai-risk-management-final.pdf

1.3 Under the Hood – Anatomy of an Agent

An enterprise-grade agent is not just an LLM with a shell script. Picture five tightly-coupled layers:

1. **Sense** – API feeds from core ledgers, market data, sat-imagery, customer speech.

2. **Remember** – Vector stores for unstructured embeddings; relational DBs for facts; graph DBs for relationships.

3. **Reason** – LLM + domain models + symbolic rules orchestrated by chain-of-thought planner.

4. **Act** – Secure function calls: initiate payment, open trade, send email, generate PDF.

5. **Govern** – Policy engine enforces limits; every step logs to an immutable ledger (often on enterprise-grade DLT) for level-three audit.

Side note: Virtually every catastrophic AI failure in the last two years occurred because step 5 was missing or bolted on as an after-thought.

By chaining existing microservices, many banks built their first pilot in <6 weeks.

1.4 Meet the Early Movers

In the relentless race to harness AI's promise, a select group of institutions has already sprinted ahead—deploying autonomous agents not as isolated experiments, but as integrated engines of growth and resilience. From freeing a billion in capital at DBS to channelling US$12 billion into new IndexGPT portfolios at JPMorgan[8], these "early movers" have set the bar for what tightly governed, outcome-driven AI can achieve. They didn't stumble upon success by chance: each created a lean "AI control tower," codified rigorous policies, and empowered dedicated squads to spin up mission-focused agents, all aligned to crystal-clear ROE or NPS targets.

As we peer into their playbooks, a common blueprint emerges. AXA Climate's weather-data agents slash claims payouts to under thirty minutes, collapsing adjuster costs by 70 percent. Starling Bank's fraud-detection agents raise the bar on protection—blocking 65 percent more illicit transactions with half the false positives and saving over £20 million in operating expenses. What unites them isn't just cutting-edge technology, but an enterprise-wide commitment to embed autonomy within well-defined guardrails. In this section, we'll explore how these trailblazers built their AI foundations—and what their early victories reveal about the next frontier of agent-driven finance.

- **DBS Bank** uses 400+ liquidity-optimisation agents. Result: S$1 bn capital freed and a +2 pp ROE uptick.

- **JPMorgan IndexGPT** offers agent-built portfolios at 40 bps all-in, pulling in US$12 bn net new assets in six months.

- **AXA Climate** pays parametric claims in <30 min thanks to weather-data agents—cutting adjuster cost 70 percent.

- **Starling Bank (UK)**: card-fraud agent blocks 65 percent more fraud than legacy rules with half the false positives, saving £20 m OPEX annually.

8 https://www.finextra.com/newsarticle/44096/jpmorgan-unveils-indexgpt-investing-tool

What they share: a small "AI control tower", rigorous policy-as-code, and product squads empowered to spin up agents against clear ROE or NPS targets.

1.5 Risks of Standing Still

There is a significant strategic risk for not acting. Financial Institutions must form a view as to what are their responses to the disruption? What is their position regarding the 4 below risks?

1. **Cost risk** — Agents drive marginal cost toward zero; manual shops will keep bleeding and likely die by a thousand cuts.

2. **Trust risk** — Customers recalibrate expectations around transparency, speed, and customisation. Non differentiated, black box offering will lose public trust in favour of nimble and customer centric competitors.

3. **Regulatory risk** — Regulators will soon deem unmanaged autonomous processes equivalent to unsafe aircraft parts.

4. **Data-network risk** — Early movers will capture feedback loops that continuously refine models—leaving laggards with stale data.

An Institute of International Finance survey of 120 CROs found 68 percent fear "uncontrolled agent proliferation" more than cyberbreach, yet 54 percent still lack any board-approved policy. Doing nothing is the riskiest option of all.

Key Take-Aways

The key takeaway is clear: Agentic AI is not about better chat—it's about better outcomes. These intelligent systems sense context, make decisions, and execute autonomously, unlocking tangible gains in Return on Equity (ROE), capital efficiency, and operational expenditure (OPEX) for forward-looking financial institutions. But the real differentiator lies in how you scale. Winners don't run isolated pilots—they embed AI into their DNA through policy-as-code frameworks and a disciplined agent operating rhythm that ensures consistent delivery, governance, and adaptability across the enterprise.

- **Agentic AI equals outcomes, not chat.** It senses context, decides, and executes.
- Financial institutions already pocket real ROE, capital, and OPEX gains.
- Winning requires policy-as-code and an "agent operating rhythm," not one-off pilots.

Next-Step Checklist (C-Suite)

To rapidly operationalize Agentic AI at scale, organizations must adopt a structured, time-bound transformation agenda. In the first two weeks, the Chief Operating Officer (COO) and Operations Strategy team should identify the top 50 high-frequency, high-effort decisions—those consuming more than 1,000 full-time equivalent hours. This insight sets the foundation for the Head of Digital and Risk to conduct a 30-day 'Agent Feasibility Sprint,' validating the decision-making patterns most suitable for autonomous agents. Within four weeks, the Chief Information Officer (CIO) and Chief Risk Officer (CRO) must co-author an 'Agent Charter'—a governing document that defines autonomy thresholds, safety guardrails, and escalation pathways. By week six, the Chief Financial Officer (CFO) should activate an AI Control Tower staffed with 5 to 7 FTEs to orchestrate early use cases and ensure observability across agent actions. Finally, within eight weeks, the Chief Human Resources Officer (CHRO) must refresh the talent blueprint, prioritizing the recruitment and development of agent orchestrators and AI-aligned risk stewards. This phased road-map ensures momentum, governance, and human-machine synergy from the outset.

Priority	Action	Who Owns	Timeframe
1	Map top-50 repetitive decisions (>1 000 FTE h)	COO + Ops Strategy	2 weeks
2	Run a 30-day 'Agent Feasibility Sprint' on one decision	Head Digital + Risk	1 month
3	Draft an 'Agent Charter' (autonomy levels, guard-rails)	CIO + CRO	4 weeks
4	Spin up an AI Control Tower (5-7 FTE to start)	CFO (budget)	6 weeks
5	Refresh talent plan (agent-orchestrator, risk lead)	CHRO	8 weeks

CHAPTER 2 – Demystifying AI Complexity: Cutting Through the Noise

In a near future, business review headline will read: *(the following statement is purely illustrative, and the person and Bank cited are fictional)*

"Our board meetings used to stall on jargon—now we frame every AI proposal as a 'decision cost' question. It changed the conversation from hype to value in one quarter." — **Luis Martínez, Chair, Andean Mutual Group**

Most executives don't suffer from *lack* of AI information—they drown in it. Vendor decks promise "transformative LLMs," regulators warn about "black-box bias," and internal teams pitch three-letter innovations weekly. This chapter arms you with a pragmatic filter: five lenses that strip away complexity and spotlight **only the AI investments that compound value and trust.**

Opening Vignette – The Five-Slide Epiphany

London, February 2025. Andean Mutual's board review spirals: 14 AI initiatives, seven tech stacks, and $22 million in sunk proofs-of-concept. The chair calls time. "Bring me five slides," he says, "one per decision class we make, map the cost of getting them wrong. Then tell me which AI narrows that cost fastest." Three weeks later, 10 projects die; four double in funding—including an agentic KYC module that will recoup compliance penalties in under a year. Complexity wasn't inevitable; it just needed reframing.

2.1 The Complexity Mirage

In the business world, it's easy to mistake the sheer number of options on the table (what we call "variety") or the breakneck pace of change ("velocity") for true complexity—but they're really just surface noise. Genuine complexity arises only when the connections between cause and effect become so tangled that it's no longer clear which inputs will lead to which outcomes. In that fog of uncertainty, strategy stalls. Yet with AI, there's a powerful antidote: peel back the layers and clearly map the chain from raw data, through predictive models, into concrete decisions—and finally, into measurable value. Once you illuminate those cause-and-effect pathways, what once seemed intractable complexity transforms into a strategic playbook. AI doesn't just automate the mundane; it brings transparency to the decision-making process, enabling leaders to see exactly how each data point flows into insights, actions, and ultimately, bottom-line impact.

Five Lenses to Slice Complexity

Lens	Core Question	Quick Diagnostic	Pay-off
1 Decision Cost	What is the $/bps impact of a wrong or late decision?	Rank top-100 decisions by P&L swing	90% of AI ROI hides in top-20 decisions
2 Data Leverage	Do we own proprietary data that improves as we scale?	Plot data uniqueness vs. refresh rate	Filters out generic use-cases
3 Cycle Time	How long from data capture to customer impact?	Map latency minutes->days	Sets agent autonomy target

4 Governance Load	What explain-ability depth do regulators demand?	Match decision to risk tier (color code)	Prevents audit drownings
5 Learning Flywheel	Does the decision emit new data that improves the model?	Draw feedback loops	Identifies com-pounding edges

Rule of Thumb: If a use-case scores high on at least three lenses, it merits pilot funding; two or fewer—archive it.

2.2 Unpacking the AI Stack in Plain English

In the architecture of an AI-driven enterprise, capabilities cannot be treated as a single, undifferentiated block—think of them instead as a meticulously layered cake, where every stratum must hold its shape or the entire structure will collapse. At the foundation sits the **Data Fabric**: the streaming pipelines, batch processes, and modern lake-house repositories that capture, cleanse, and catalog your raw inputs. Without robust governance and a clear metadata catalogue, even the most sophisticated models will starve for quality fuel.

Above that, the **Foundation Models** layer provides the generative engines—large language models, diffusion networks, and time-series transformers—that learn patterns and extract latent insights at scale. But these leviathans of AI are only as useful as the context in which they're deployed, which brings us to the middle tier: **Domain Adaptors**. Here, fine-tuning and retrieval-augmented generation (RAG) temper general-purpose models with industry-specific data and workflows, transforming raw intelligence into actionable expertise.

Next, the **Decision Orchestrators** layer coordinates the flow of thought: chaining reasoning steps, executing vector searches for relevant precedents, and applying embedded rule engines to ensure every recommendation aligns with your governance framework. This is where AI begins to mirror human judgment—planning strategies, weighing constraints, and proposing multi-path scenarios for leadership to evaluate.

Finally, at the top of the stack, the **Action & Ledger** tier ensures that every decision seamlessly translates into secure execution and immutable record-keeping. Secure APIs trigger microservices and event buses, while an audit-grade blockchain or distributed ledger captures an indelible history of what was decided, who approved it, and when. Neglect any one of these layers, and the frosting of seamless autonomy will slide right off proving that in a well-engineered AI ecosystem, strength truly comes from the strength of each individual layer.

2.3 Common Complexity Traps—and How to Escape

Agentic AI initiatives often stall not due to ambition, but because of four predictable traps. "Pilot Paralysis" is the graveyard of good intentions—when 25 proof-of-concepts (POCs) yield zero production. The fix? Kill 70%, and force the survivors to absorb full cloud OPEX, creating economic accountability. In the "Vendor Vortex," tech debt spirals as firms juggle multiple ML platforms; the escape is to enforce a single, open-standards backbone with clear vendor exit clauses. "Metric Mirage" misleads teams into chasing elusive 99% model accuracy—redirect them to track decision value instead: dollars saved per claim, or basis points of ROE uplifted. Lastly, "Compliance Catch-up" burns reputations when audit issues arise post-launch. Avoid it by adopting a "shift left" mindset—where policy-as-code is embedded before model code is even written.

Trap	Symptom	Escape Move
"Pilot Paralysis"	25 POCs, no production	Kill 70 %, force remaining POCs to carry full cloud cost in OPEX forecast
"Vendor Vortex"	Tech debt balloons, seven ML platforms	Mandate one open-standards backbone, require exit clauses
"Metric Mirage"	Teams chase 99 % model accuracy	Switch to *decision-value* metrics: $ saved / claim, bps ROE gained
"Compliance Catch-up"	Audit findings post-launch	Shift to *shift-left* governance—policy code built before model code

2.4 Case in Point - Simplifying KYC at Andean Mutual

- In the high-stakes world of financial crime prevention, every decision carries a tangible price tag—and every inefficiency drags on the bottom line. Consider the true cost of "false positives": each one demands a manual review, ringing up roughly $27 per case and tallying nearly $2 million in annual labour alone. Yet the organization sits atop a strategic gold-mine—twelve years of archived customer behaviour data that few rivals can match—offering a rare advantage in pattern recognition and anomaly detection. The current cycle time for investigations stretches 48 hours; the goal is to slash that to just four minutes, moving from a two-day lag to near-instantaneous insight. All of this must take place under the exacting scrutiny of FATF guidelines and Europe's AMLD6 regulations, where full explainability isn't optional but mandatory.

- Enter the learning flywheel: every false alarm that's cleared by an investigator automatically becomes new training data, refining the model's accuracy and reducing future review costs. The payoff speaks for itself—a single, well-engineered agent module drove an 82 percent drop in manual reviews, translating to $1.6 million in savings within just nine months. What made that win possible wasn't some arcane breakthrough in model architecture, but relentless complexity management—aligning cost, data, speed, governance, and continuous learning into a cohesive, self-reinforcing system.

2.5 Measuring What Matters: The Agentic ROI Framework

The era of vague AI promises has ended. Boards demand concrete metrics, regulators require quantifiable risk assessments, and shareholders expect measurable returns. Leading banks have developed sophisticated frameworks for measuring agentic AI impact, moving beyond simple cost savings to capture value creation across multiple dimensions.

The Four-Tier Measurement Hierarchy

Tier 1: Operational Metrics (The Fundamentals)

These metrics provide immediate feedback on system performance and form the foundation for all other measurements:

Decision Velocity:

- **Definition:** Time from data availability to decision execution
- **Targets by Domain:**
  - Trading decisions: <10 milliseconds (competitive advantage disappears at 100ms)
  - Fraud detection: <100 milliseconds (before transaction clears)
  - Credit decisions: <5 seconds (customer abandonment rises after 10 seconds)
  - Customer service: <2 seconds (perceived as "instant" by humans)
- **Measurement Method:** End-to-end tracing with correlation IDs
- **JPMorgan Achievement:** Reduced credit decision time from 6 hours to 7 minutes

Automation Rate:

- **Definition:** Percentage of decisions made without human intervention

- **Current Industry Performance:**
  - Document processing: 85-95% (structured documents)
  - Customer service: 70-80% (routine inquiries)
  - Fraud detection: 60-70% (with human review for edge cases)
  - Trading execution: 95-99% (algorithmic trading)
- **Measurement Challenges:** Defining "decision" consistently across domains.
- **HSBC Achievement:** 90% automation in AML transaction monitoring

Error Reduction:

- **Types of Errors Tracked:**
  - False positives (unnecessary alerts/blocks)
  - False negatives (missed issues)
  - Processing errors (system failures)
  - Compliance violations (regulatory breaches)
- **Baseline Establishment:** Compare to pre-AI error rates.
- **Statistical Significance:** Minimum 6-month comparison period
- **HSBC Result:** 45% reduction in AML false positives, saving 10,000 investigation hours monthly.

Cost per Decision:

- **Full Cost Accounting Includes:**
  - Infrastructure (compute, storage, network): J0.001-0.01 per decision
  - Model API calls: J0.01-0.10 per decision.
  - Human oversight: J1-50 per escalation
  - Compliance/audit: J0.10-1 per decision
- **Traditional Comparison:** Human processing costs J10-500 per decision
- **Target Reduction:** 90-95% cost reduction versus human processing
- **Morgan Stanley Achievement:** Reduced cost per client interaction from J45 to J2

Tier 2: Business Metrics (The Value Drivers)

These metrics connect operational improvements to business outcomes:

Revenue per Employee:

- **Calculation:** Total revenue / FTE count
- **AI Impact Measurement:** Compare departments with/without AI deployment.

- **Industry Leaders:**
  - JPMorgan: $500K revenue per employee (up 15% since AI deployment)
  - Goldman Sachs: $1.2M revenue per employee in trading (up 25%)
- **Attribution Challenge:** Isolating AI contribution from other factors

Customer Satisfaction (NPS):

- **AI-Specific Measurements:**
  - NPS for AI-assisted interactions vs traditional
  - Resolution rate on first contact
  - Customer effort score
  - Sentiment analysis of feedback
- **Bank of America Achievement:** Erica users show 15-point higher NPS.
- **Critical Insight:** Speed improvement drives satisfaction more than accuracy.

Market Share Growth:

- **Digital-Native Segments:** Banks with superior AI capture 2-3x market share
- **Product-Specific Gains:**
  - Digital lending: 40% share growth for AI leaders
  - Robo-advisory: 60% asset growth for personalised AI platforms

    - SME banking: 35% growth through automated services
- **Competitive Intelligence:** Monitor competitor AI deployments and market response.

Risk-Adjusted Returns (ROE/RAROC):

- **Direct Contributions:**
    - Lower operational costs: 100-200 bps ROE improvement
    - Better risk selection: 50-150 bps from reduced defaults
    - Capital efficiency: 50-100 bps from optimised allocation.
    - Revenue growth: 100-200 bps from new products/markets
- **JPMorgan Target:** 17% ROE by 2027 (from 15% baseline)

Tier 3: Strategic Metrics (The Differentiators)

These forward-looking metrics indicate long-term competitive advantage:

Innovation Velocity:

- **Metrics:**
    - Time from concept to production: Target <90 days
    - Number of experiments per quarter: Leading banks run 100+
    - Percentage of experiments graduated to production: Target >20%
    - Reusability rate of AI components: Target >70%
- **Platform Effect:** Each successful deployment accelerates the next

Talent Leverage:

- **Productivity Multipliers:**
  - Data scientists supporting 10x more models with MLOps.
  - Business analysts creating models without engineering support.
  - Relationship managers serving 2x clients with AI support.
- **Skill Evolution:** Track percentage of workforce using AI tools daily.

Regulatory Efficiency:

- **Compliance Metrics:**
  - Reduction in regulatory findings: 50-70% fewer issues
  - Remediation cost reduction: 40-60% through automation
  - Time to compliance for new regulations: 3 months vs 12 months traditional
  - Audit preparation time: Reduced by 80%
- **Proactive Compliance:** Predict and prevent violations before they occur.

Platform Extensibility:

- **Reuse Metrics:**
  - Number of use cases per core capability
  - Time to deploy new use case on existing platform.
  - Percentage of code reused across applications.

- **Network Effects:** Each new application makes the next one easier.

Tier 4: Risk and Governance Metrics (The Guardrails)

These metrics ensure sustainable and responsible growth:

Model Risk Indicators:

- **Drift Metrics:**
  - Feature drift: Statistical distribution changes in inputs
  - Concept drift: Relationship changes between inputs and outputs
  - Performance drift: Degradation in accuracy metrics
- **Threshold Management:** Automated alerts when drift exceeds limits.

Bias and Fairness Metrics:

- **Measurements Across Protected Classes:**
  - Demographic parity: Equal positive rates across groups
  - Equalised odds: Equal error rates across groups
  - Individual fairness: Similar treatment for similar individuals
- **Continuous Monitoring:** Daily bias scans across all models

Operational Risk Metrics:

- **System Reliability:**
    - Availability: Target 99.95% uptime
    - Latency: P99 within SLA requirements
    - Error rates: <0.1% system errors
- **Concentration Risk:** Avoid over-reliance on single models/ vendors.

The Executive Dashboard

Leading banks synthesise these metrics into executive dashboards updated in real-time:

JPMorgan's AI Control Tower:

```
═══════════════════════════════════════════
        AI OPERATIONS DASHBOARD
        Updated: 2025-01-30 14:30 UTC
═══════════════════════════════════════════

OPERATIONAL HEALTH
├─ Active Agents: 1,247 (↑ 15%)
├─ Decisions Today: 45.2M (on track)
├─ Avg Latency: 127ms (✓ within SLA)
└─ Error Rate: 0.03% (✓ below threshold)

BUSINESS IMPACT (MTD)
├─ Cost Savings: $47M (112% of target)
├─ Revenue Attribution: $123M (95% of target)
├─ NPS Delta: +12 points (above baseline)
└─ ROE Contribution: 187 bps

RISK INDICATORS
├─ Model Drift: 2 models flagged (investigating)
├─ Bias Alerts: 0 (last alert: 7 days ago)
├─ Regulatory Flags: 0
└─ Vendor Concentration: 34% (✓ below 40% limit)

STRATEGIC PROGRESS
├─ New Capabilities: 7 launched this month
├─ Experiments Active: 47
├─ Talent Utilisation: 67% using AI daily
└─ Platform Reuse: 73% component sharing
═══════════════════════════════════════════
```

ROI Calculation Methodology

The most sophisticated challenge is calculating true ROI, accounting for both direct and indirect effects:

Direct Benefits (Easily Quantifiable):

- Cost reduction from automation
- Revenue from new AI products
- Efficiency gains in processing time
- Error reduction savings

Indirect Benefits (Harder to Measure):

- Customer lifetime value improvement
- Brand value from innovation leadership
- Employee satisfaction from eliminating mundane tasks.
- Option value of AI platform for future uses

Total Cost Consideration:

- Initial development costs
- Ongoing operational expenses
- Governance and compliance costs
- Opportunity cost of capital
- Risk-adjusted cost of failures.

JPMorgan's ROI Calculation:

- **Annual AI Investment:** $2B
- **Direct Cost Savings:** $1.2B
- **Revenue Attribution:** $1.5B
- **Risk Reduction Value:** $300M.
- **Gross ROI:** 150% (3B return on 2B investment)
- **Risk-Adjusted ROI:** 95% (after failure costs and risk provisions)

This comprehensive measurement framework transforms AI from an experiment to an operational discipline, enabling continuous improvement and justifying continued investment.

Key Take-Aways

Complexity in Agentic AI isn't inevitable—it's a choice. Leaders can cut through the noise by applying five focused lenses to structure decisions and scale with clarity. The real leverage point lies in decision orchestration and policy-as-code—this is where audit risk concentrates and where resilience is built. Finally, to escape "pilot paralysis," stop subsidizing indecision. Charge AI initiatives full operational expenditure and demand they prove value in business terms: decisions made, dollars saved, and ROE gained.

- Complexity ≠ inevitable; use five lenses to slice the noise.
- Over-invest in decision orchestration and policy-as-code—where audit risk lives.
- Kill "pilot paralysis" by charging projects real OPEX and tracking decision value.

Next-Step Checklist (C-Suite)

To move from intent to impact, the C-suite must act decisively. Start with a Decision Cost workshop, led by the CFO and CRO, to rank the top 20 decisions by frequency and value—this creates a clear investment map within two weeks. Next, within three weeks, the CIO and Strategy team must score all existing AI initiatives using the five-lens framework, surfacing where complexity hides or value leaks. Armed with this clarity, the CEO should, in week four, cut or consolidate low-scoring pilots—no exceptions. Finally, appoint a policy-as-code architect under Risk IT to build Layer 5 governance scaffolding. This role is critical for aligning execution with regulatory readiness and long-term trust.

Priority	**Action**	**Owner**	**Timeframe**
1	Run Decision-Cost workshop; rank top-20 decisions	CFO + CRO	2 weeks
2	Perform five-lens scoring on all AI initiatives	CIO + Strategy	3 weeks
3	Cut or merge low-scoring pilots	CEO endorsement	1 week
4	Assign policy-as-code architect for layer-5 governance	Head of Risk IT	4 weeks

So What & Call to Action

So What?

The complexity often associated with AI is largely a mirage—noise that dissipates once organizations begin slicing their initiatives through five practical lenses. When viewed through the filters of decision cost, data leverage, cycle time, governance load, and learning flywheel, clarity emerges. This structured approach reveals where real value lies and where waste accumulates. The truth is, only a fraction—typically the top 20%—of your decision inventory drives the majority of business value. Conversely, the bulk of compliance and audit friction doesn't stem from model performance but from gaps in policy orchestration, oversight, and execution discipline.

AI at scale is a decision architecture challenge, not just a model engineering exercise. And yet, many organizations stay trapped in pilot purgatory or overinvest in the model lab while underinvesting in the governance layer—where regulators focus and risk lives. Without clear decision prioritization and proactive governance scaffolding, even technically impressive models deliver disappointing business results or audit blowback.

Call to action:

The call to action for the next 90 days is both practical and urgent.

First, run a cross-functional sprint to identify and rank the top 20 high-impact, high-frequency decisions in your business. Prioritize based on effort, volume, and value—this is your target zone for Agentic AI.

Second, apply the five-lens framework to all current AI projects. Projects that score low across these dimensions—particularly on decision value or governance readiness—should be cut, merged, or paused. These are often the sources of complexity without return.

Third, shift funding away from vanity AI and toward the invisible layers that drive measurable impact—decision orchestration and policy as code. These are the levers regulators and boards care about and where audit risk lives or dies.

Fourth, appoint an AI Governance Architect responsible for embedding policy YAML templates, automated edge-case tests, and live monitoring dashboards—*before* any new model code is written. This "shift left" mindset bakes trust, fairness, and auditability into your AI fabric from day one.

Taken together, these four moves won't just de-risk your AI roadmap—they'll operationalize it. You'll translate AI noise into measurable ROE uplift, slash audit anxiety, and unlock capacity for genuinely high-value innovation. This is how you shift from AI ambition to enterprise-grade execution.

CHAPTER 3 – From Generative to Agentic: The Stack & The Maturity Curve

"The more people get deep into it and unlock what it's good at and what it's not, the more we're starting to see the ideas really flourishing."
Teresa Heitsenrether, CDAO, JPMorgan Chase[9]

Generative AI wowed boards with human-like prose and code. Yet many early pilots plateaued at "content creation" because they lacked two ingredients: **tool access** and **governance-by-design**. When you give models-controlled levers—payments APIs, trading gateways, client comms channels—and bind them to policy code, you cross the line into **agentic intelligence**. This chapter maps the journey: the technology stack you need, the maturity curve that boards should track, and the integration patterns that separate demos from dollars.

Use Case – JPMorgan Chase: The Full-Stack Pioneer

Summary:

- JPMorgan Chase loan processing
- Their Contract Intelligence (COiN) system processing loan agreements in seconds vs hours
- The 30-second investment banking deck creation demonstration
- Real metrics: 360,000 hours saved annually.

9 https://www.forbes.com/sites/randybean/2025/07/27/at-jpmorganchase-ai-innovation-is-an-operating-committee-mandate/

JPMorgan Chase is undergoing what executives describe as a "fundamental rewiring" for the AI era. Their vision extends beyond automation to complete transformation: every employee equipped with AI agents, every back-office process automated, and every client interaction enhanced by AI concierges. This isn't marketing rhetoric—it's a $18 billion annual technology investment strategy with clear deliverables and measurable outcomes.

The LLM Suite Platform: Initially launched to 60,000 employees and now available to over 140,000 staff members globally, LLM Suite serves as JPMorgan's proprietary portal for accessing large language models. Rather than developing proprietary models—a costly and risky endeavour—the bank created an intelligent abstraction layer that can tap into models from OpenAI, Anthropic, and other providers. This approach provides flexibility whilst avoiding vendor lock-in. As Teresa Heitsenrether, their Chief Data and Analytics Officer, explains: "The plan is not to be beholden to any one model provider. We want to move fluidly across models depending on use cases."

The platform isn't just a chatbot interface. Employees use it for complex tasks including:

- Writing and summarising lengthy documents (reducing report creation time by 70%)
- Problem-solving with Excel and data analysis (catching errors human analysts miss)
- Generating ideas for marketing campaigns and product innovations
- Creating code and debugging applications (developers report 40% productivity gains)
- Analysing customer feedback and identifying patterns across millions of interactions

Measurable Impact: The numbers tell a compelling story. The bank's Contract Intelligence (COiN) system processes commercial loan agreements in seconds rather than hours, eliminating 360,000 hours of legal work annually—equivalent to 180 full-time employees. In a demonstration to journalists, their AI platform created a comprehensive investment banking pitch deck in 30 seconds, complete with market analysis, comparable transactions, and valuation ranges—work that previously required a team of junior bankers working through the night.

Customer service transformation has been equally dramatic. AI-powered systems now handle millions of routine enquiries, freeing human agents to focus on complex, high-value interactions. The bank reports that customers using AI-assisted channels show 15% higher satisfaction scores and 25% lower call-back rates, indicating problems are being resolved correctly the first time.

Infrastructure Investment: JPMorgan's commitment goes beyond software. The bank will spend $18 billion on technology in 2025, up from $17 billion in 2024. Critically, they've modernised their infrastructure foundation: 65% of workloads now run on public or private cloud platforms, up from 50% a year ago. When including applications on virtual servers, that number reaches 80%. This cloud transformation wasn't just about cost—it was about creating the elastic compute infrastructure necessary for AI workloads that can spike 100x during peak processing periods.

The bank has also invested heavily in data architecture. Managing 500 petabytes of data requires industrial-scale systems. They've implemented a modern data lakehouse architecture combining structured and unstructured data, with sophisticated lineage tracking ensuring they can trace any AI decision back to its source data—crucial for regulatory compliance.

Organisational Transformation: Technology alone doesn't drive change—people do. JPMorgan has restructured entire departments around AI capabilities. They've created an AI Centre of Excellence with over 200 data scientists and ML engineers, but more importantly, they've embedded AI expertise within business units. Every major department now has dedicated "AI Champions" who bridge technical and business domains.

Training has been massive in scale: over 40,000 employees have completed AI literacy programmes, 5,000 have received advanced prompt engineering training, and 500 business analysts have been reskilled as "citizen data scientists" capable of building and deploying simple models without engineering support.

3.1 Three Waves of Automation

Across three successive waves of intelligent automation, organizations have steadily expanded the scope and impact of their digital workforce. From 2015 to 2019, RPA paired with basic machine learning set out to "automate the swivel chair," driving significant cost reductions by replacing manual, repetitive tasks with tools like UiPath and scikit-learn. Between 2020 and 2023, the rise of generative AI shifted the focus to "automate the draft," boosting content productivity through powerful models such as GPT-3/4 and Stable Diffusion. Today, the emerging era of agentic AI takes a leap beyond task and content automation to "automate the outcome," where integrated large language models, policy engines, and event buses work in concert to accelerate decision velocity and capital efficiency.

Wave	Motto	Value Ceiling	Typical Tools
RPA & ML (2015-19)	"Automate the swivel-chair"	Cost take-out	UiPath, scikit-learn
Generative AI (2020-23)	"Automate the draft"	Content productivity	GPT-3/4, Stable Diffusion
Agentic AI (2024-)	"Automate the outcome"	Decision velocity & capital efficiency	LLM+tools, policy engines, event busses

Each wave builds on the last. Boards must avoid investing in wave-2 pilots when competitors are leaping to wave-3 platforms.

3.1.1 The Current AI Landscape - Where We Stand in 2025

The agentic AI revolution has accelerated far beyond initial projections. As we write in mid-2025, the landscape has fundamentally shifted from experimental pilots to production deployments at scale. JPMorgan Chase now provides its LLM Suite platform to over 200,000 employees globally, with users reporting productivity gains of several hours per week through automated report generation, code development, and data analysis tasks. This isn't theoretical—its operational reality delivering measurable ROI that CFOs can track quarterly.

The current model ecosystem has evolved dramatically. Claude Opus 4.1 and Sonnet 4 from Anthropic now demonstrate advanced reasoning capabilities that surpass GPT-4's initial benchmarks by 40% on complex financial analysis tasks, particularly excelling in multi-step reasoning and maintaining context across lengthy documents. OpenAI's o1 reasoning models have introduced chain-of-thought transparency that regulators increasingly demand—showing their working in a way that satisfies audit requirements. Google's Gemini 2.0 has become the de facto standard for multimodal document processing in KYC workflows, capable of extracting data from handwritten forms, scanned documents, and even video calls with 98% accuracy. Meta's Llama 3.1, with its 405 billion parameter version, provides the open-source alternative many institutions require for on-premises deployment, particularly in jurisdictions with strict data residency requirements.

The shift from single agents to multi-agent orchestration represents the most significant architectural evolution of 2025. Enterprises now deploy sophisticated orchestration systems where multiple specialised agents collaborate on complex tasks. A typical loan approval process might involve a credit assessment agent, a fraud detection agent, a document verification agent, and a compliance checking agent—all coordinating through a master orchestrator that ensures consistency and completeness. Microsoft's Azure AI Foundry Agent Service now provides enterprise-grade multi-agent capabilities with built-in observability for tracking performance, cost, and safety metrics in real-time. Open-source frameworks like AutoGen (from Microsoft Research), CrewAI, and LangChain have matured from experimental tools to production-ready platforms, with major banks running thousands of agent interactions daily through these systems.

The Numbers That Matter: JPMorgan Chase delivered more than $1.5 billion in business value from AI and machine learning in 2023, leveraging 500 petabytes of data across 300 use cases in production. By 2025, they're targeting $2 billion in AI-related upside through expanded deployment of their LLM Suite and autonomous agent systems. Their Contract Intelligence platform alone has eliminated 360,000 hours of manual document review annually. This scale of implementation requires not just technology but fundamental organisational transformation—from how teams are structured to how success is measured.

The global agentic AI tools market has exploded from $6.67 billion in 2024 to a projected $10.41 billion in 2025, representing a compound annual growth rate of 56.1%. This growth isn't speculative—it's driven by measurable business outcomes. Banks report 30% reductions in operational costs, 80% faster decision-making in structured domains, and customer satisfaction improvements of 10-15 NPS points where agentic systems have been deployed effectively.

3.2 The Agentic Tech Stack - 2025 Reality

The theoretical orchestra has become an operational reality. After analysing implementations across leading banks, clear patterns emerge in the technology choices and architecture decisions that separate success from struggle. Here's how institutions actually build their stacks, with specific technologies and hard-won lessons from production deployments.

Layer 1: Data Fabric (The Foundation)

The data layer determines everything—get it wrong, and no amount of AI sophistication can save you. JPMorgan manages 500 petabytes of data, HSBC processes 375 million transactions monthly, and Morgan Stanley analyses 100,000 research documents. This scale requires industrial-grade infrastructure:

Streaming Backbone:

- **Apache Kafka/Confluent:** 90% of banks use Kafka for event streaming. JPMorgan processes 7 trillion messages annually through their Kafka clusters.

- **Amazon Kinesis/Azure Event Hubs:** Cloud-native alternatives for firms avoiding infrastructure management.

- **Apache Pulsar:** Emerging alternative offering better multi-tenancy and geo-replication.

- **Real-world throughput:** Leading banks process 2-5 million events per second at peak

Critical lesson: Don't underestimate streaming infrastructure. Banks report 60% of initial AI projects fail due to data pipeline issues, not model problems.

Lakehouse Architecture:

- **Databricks:** Dominant platform, used by 8 of top 10 banks. Provides unified analytics with Delta Lake for ACID transactions on data lakes.

- **Snowflake:** Strong alternative, particularly for SQL-heavy workloads. Excellent data sharing capabilities for multi-party scenarios.

- **AWS Lake Formation/Azure Synapse:** Cloud-native options with tight integration to respective clouds

- **Apache Iceberg:** Open table format gaining traction for vendor independence.

Implementation reality: Most banks run hybrid architectures. Example from HSBC:

- Historical data in Snowflake (500TB+)

- Real-time streams in Kafka (2M events/second)

- Feature computation in Databricks (10,000 features updated hourly)
- Model training data in S3/Delta Lake (50TB active training sets)

Feature Stores:

- **Tecton:** Purpose-built feature platform with point-in-time correctness for training
- **Feast:** Open-source option with strong community support
- **AWS SageMaker Feature Store:** Integrated with AWS ML stack.
- **Databricks Feature Store:** Native integration with MLflow and Delta Lake

The feature store revelation: Banks initially resisted feature stores as unnecessary complexity. Those that adopted them report 70% reduction in model development time and virtual elimination of training-serving skew.

Vector Databases:

- **Pinecone:** Managed service with superior performance for large-scale deployments
- **Weaviate:** Open-source with excellent hybrid search capabilities
- **Qdrant:** High-performance option with on-premises deployment options
- **Milvus:** Open-source, battle-tested at scale by Chinese banks

Scaling realities: Vector databases become bottlenecks at scale. Solutions:

- Hierarchical indexing (coarse-to-fine retrieval)
- Caching frequent queries (80% of queries are repeated)
- Partitioning by business domain (customer service vs trading)
- Typical scale: 10-100 billion vectors with sub-100ms query times

Layer 2: Model Layer (The Intelligence)

The model landscape changes monthly, but patterns in production deployments have stabilised:

Commercial Models (The Workhorses):

- **OpenAI GPT-4o:** 45% of production workloads. Excellent for general reasoning and code generation. Average latency: 500ms-2s
- **Anthropic Claude Opus 4.1:** 30% of workloads. Superior for long documents and complex reasoning. Better adherence to instructions.
- **Google Gemini 2.0:** 15% of workloads. Best multimodal performance for document processing. Native Google Workspace integration.
- **Cohere Command R+:** 10% of workloads. Excellent retrieval augmentation and multilingual support.

Cost reality: At scale, model costs are substantial. JPMorgan spends an estimated $50M annually on API calls. Optimisation strategies:

- Semantic caching reduces costs by 40%.
- Routing simple queries to smaller models saves 60%.
- Batch processing non-urgent requests cuts costs by 30%.

Open Models (The Control Option):

- **Meta Llama 3.1 (405B):** Best open-source option for complex reasoning. Requires 8x A100 GPUs for inference.
- **Mistral Large 2:** European alternative with strong multilingual performance
- **Qwen 2.5:** Emerging option with excellent benchmark scores
- **Falcon 180B:** Popular in Middle East due to Arabic optimisation

Deployment realities: Open models aren't "free"—infrastructure costs often exceed API costs:

- 405B parameter model: $500K+ annual infrastructure cost
- 70B parameter model: $100K+ annual infrastructure cost
- 7B parameter model: $10K+ annual infrastructure cost
- Factor in GPUs, networking, storage, cooling, management overhead.

Specialised Models (The Domain Experts):

- **Bloomberg GPT:** Financial language understanding, trained on 50 years of financial data.
- **FinBERT:** Sentiment analysis on financial text, 93% accuracy on earnings calls
- **TimeGPT:** Time series forecasting, outperforms traditional methods by 20-30%
- **TabPFN:** Tabular data prediction, superior to XGBoost on small datasets

Small Language Models for Edge (The Speed Demons):

- **Microsoft Phi-3:** 3.8B parameters, runs on mobile devices, 80% of GPT-4 capability.
- **Google Gemma 2B:** Optimised for on-device deployment, 50ms latency.
- **Apple OpenELM:** Designed for iOS devices, privacy-preserving.
- **Custom Distilled Models:** Banks create domain-specific 1-2B parameter models.

Edge deployment statistics:

- 90% accuracy retention with 10x size reduction
- 50ms inference latency on branch servers

- 99.9% availability without internet connectivity
- $1,000 per location annual infrastructure cost

Layer 3: Orchestration (The Conductor)

This layer has seen the most innovation, with frameworks evolving from simple prompt chains to sophisticated multi-agent systems:

Frameworks (The Building Blocks):

LangChain (The Pioneer):

- 100+ integrations out-of-box
- Excellent documentation and community
- LangSmith for debugging and monitoring.
- Challenges: Abstraction overhead, version instability
- Production usage: 40% of banks use in some capacity.

AutoGen (The Collaborator):

- Native multi-agent support
- Human-in-the-loop capabilities
- Excellent for research/analysis tasks
- Microsoft backing ensures enterprise support.
- Production usage: Growing rapidly, 25% adoption.

CrewAI (The Specialist):

- Role-based agent design
- Hierarchical task management
- Strong async execution
- Simpler than alternatives for basic use cases
- Production usage: 20% adoption, particularly in smaller banks

Semantic Kernel (The Enterprise Choice):

- Microsoft's enterprise framework
- Native Azure integration
- Plugin architecture for extensibility
- C# and Python support
- Production usage: Dominant in Microsoft-centric organisations

Custom Frameworks: Many banks build custom orchestration layers:

- JPMorgan's internal framework handles 1M+ agent interactions daily
- HSBC's proprietary system manages regulatory complexity.
- Morgan Stanley's platform optimised for financial advisory workflows.

Workflow Engines (The Process Managers):

- **Apache Airflow:** 60% of banks use for batch workflows. Mature but showing age.
- **Prefect:** Modern alternative with better failure handling and observability
- **Temporal:** Excellent for long-running workflows with complex state
- **Dagster:** Asset-based orchestration aligns well with data pipelines.

Agent Communication (The Nervous System):

- **RabbitMQ:** Battle-tested message broker, handles millions of messages.
- **Apache Kafka:** When streaming and messaging converge.
- **NATS:** Lightweight, high-performance for simple messaging
- **gRPC:** For synchronous service-to-service communication

Communication patterns in production:

- Async messaging for resilience (95% of agent communication)
- Synchronous calls only for sub-second requirements
- Event sourcing for audit trails
- Circuit breakers prevent cascade failures.

Layer 4: Execution (The Tools)

The tool layer is where AI meets reality—connecting to systems that move money, execute trades, and serve customers:

Internal APIs (The Core Systems):

Banks expose internal capabilities through standardised APIs:

- **Core Banking:** Account management, transaction processing, balance queries.
- **Payment Rails:** ACH, SWIFT, instant payments, card networks
- **Trading Systems:** Order management, execution, settlement
- **Risk Systems:** Limits checking, exposure calculation, VAR models.
- **Customer Systems:** CRM, communication preferences, interaction history

API Gateway patterns:

- Kong/Apigee for API management
- Rate limiting prevents agent overload.
- Circuit breakers for resilience
- OAuth 2.0/mTLS for security

Typical API performance:

- Read operations: 50-200ms latency, 10,000 TPS capacity.
- Write operations: 200-500ms latency, 1,000 TPS capacity.
- Batch operations: Async processing for large updates.

External Services (The World Connection):

- **Market Data:** Bloomberg (J20K/terminal), Refinitiv (J15K/terminal), direct exchange feeds
- **Credit Bureaus:** Experian, Equifax, TransUnion APIs (J0.50-5 per query)
- **Regulatory Reporting:** Direct submission to regulators (FCA, SEC, ECB)
- **Cloud Services:** AWS Textract for OCR, Google Vision for image analysis
- **Alternative Data:** Social media sentiment, satellite imagery, web scraping

Integration challenges:

- Rate limits require careful orchestration.
- Costs can spiral without proper controls.
- Latency varies wildly (50ms to 30 seconds)
- Reliability ranges from 99.999% to 90%

Compute Resources (The Engine Room):

- **Kubernetes:** Universal standard for container orchestration. 100% of top banks use it.
- **GPU Clusters:** NVIDIA A100/H100 for training, T4/A10 for inference
- **Ray:** Distributed computing for parallel agent execution
- **Serverless:** Lambda/Functions for sporadic workloads

Resource allocation realities:

- Training: 100-1000 GPU hours per model
- Inference: 10-100 GPUs continuously for production
- Cost: J1-10M annually for infrastructure
- Utilisation: 40-60% typical (optimisation opportunity)

Layer 5: Governance (The Guardian)

The governance layer has evolved from an afterthought to a fundamental requirement:

Policy Engines (The Rule Enforcers):

- **Open Policy Agent (OPA):** Industry standard for policy as code
- **AWS Cedar:** Amazon's policy language with formal verification

- **Styra:** Commercial OPA platform with enterprise features
- **Custom DSLs:** Many banks create domain-specific policy languages.

Policy execution metrics:

- 10M+ policy evaluations daily
- <10ms evaluation latency
- 100% compliance guarantee (violations impossible)
- Version-controlled with full audit trail

Monitoring (The Watchtower):

- **Weights & Biases:** Experiment tracking and model monitoring
- **MLflow:** Open-source platform for ML lifecycle
- **Datadog/New Relic:** APM extended for AI observability.
- **Custom Dashboards:** Grafana/Kibana for business metrics

Key metrics tracked:

- Model drift: Daily statistical tests.
- Bias indicators: Real-time fairness metrics
- Business impact: Revenue/cost attribution
- Regulatory compliance: Automated report generation

Audit Logging (The Memory):

- **Immutable Ledgers:** Amazon QLDB, Azure Confidential Ledger
- **Blockchain:** Hyperledger Fabric for multi-party scenarios
- **Traditional Databases:** PostgreSQL with write-once tables.
- **Object Storage:** S3/Blob with object lock for documents.

Audit requirements:

- Every decision logged with full context
- 7-year retention minimum
- Sub-second query capability
- Cryptographic proof of non-tampering

3.3 The Agentic Maturity Curve (Organisation-Wide View)

As organizations progress from early experimentation to fully autonomous AI ecosystems, they move through five distinct stages—each defined by rising levels of autonomy, sharpened success metrics, and new operational risks to manage. At **Stage A0**, teams tinker with LLM prototypes, focusing on prompt quality as their primary KPI, but often fall prey to hype cycles and lack the infrastructure budget to scale. Moving into **Stage A1**, single-tool agents take shape with human sign-off gates; here the goal is to compress cycle-time deltas, yet manual gatekeeping frequently erodes any ROI gains. By **Stage A2**, multi-tool agents emerge under conditional approval workflows, targeting lower cost-per-outcome, though policy sprawl and tangled "tool spaghetti" can stall progress. At **Stage A3**, end-to-end agents operate within pre-defined limits, delivering measurable ROE uplift and improved NPS—but without adequate investment in observability, this sophistication can outpace an organization's ability to monitor performance and risk. Finally, **Stage A4** ushers in self-improving agent portfolios that drive capital velocity and unlock new revenue streams, though weak audit trails and regulator skepticism can threaten the very autonomy that powers their success. Across these stages, mastering the balance between autonomy, accountability, and robustness becomes the defining challenge of any AI-led transformation.

Stage	Autonomy	Success KPI	Common Pitfalls
A0	LLM prototypes	Prompt quality	Hype cycles, no infra budget
A1	Single-tool agents, human sign-off	Cycle-time delta	Manual gatekeeping kills ROI
A2	Multi-tool agents, conditional sign-off	Cost per outcome	Policy sprawl, tool spaghetti
A3	End-to-end agents within limits	ROE uplift, NPS	Under-funded observability
A4	Self-improving agent portfolios	Capital velocity, new revenue	Regulator scepticism if audit weak

Boards should ask: *What % of high-value decisions sit at each stage?* A1 is table-stakes by 2025, A3 triggers strategic advantage, A4 rewrites industry structure.

3.4 Integration Playbook - From Pilot to Platform

Every successful journey toward autonomous decision-making begins with a clear Decision Contract—an explicit definition of the desired outcome metric, acceptable tolerance bands, and a well-charted escalation path should things go awry. From there, you Abstract Tool Access by wrapping every critical function—whether that's payments, trading, CRM updates, or general-ledger entries—into a signed, centralized function registry: no registered function, no action permitted. To keep your ecosystem watertight, Embed Policy Early, storing declarative YAML rules alongside your code and running red-team tests on every commit. With the groundwork in place, make Observability First, streaming latency, model drift, and fairness indicators directly to your CRO dashboard so you can spot—and correct—issues in real time. Finally, Iterate Autonomy: as your metrics and confidence grow, gradually ease the human-in-the-loop constraints, allowing agents to take on ever more responsibility without sacrificing control.

1. **Define Decision Contract.** Outcome metric, tolerance, escalation path.

2. **Abstract Tool Access.** Wrap payments, trading, CRM, GL in signed function registry. No function = no action.

3. **Embed Policy Early.** YAML files versioned with code; red-team tests on every commit.

4. **Observability First.** Latency, drift, fairness streamed to CRO dashboard.

5. **Iterate Autonomy.** Gradually relax human-in-loop as confidence and metrics prove out.

Case Snapshot: A Tier-1 Australian bank moved card dispute resolution from A1 to A3 in nine months, cutting $14 m OPEX and boosting dispute win rate 12 pp—all after tooling wrappers and observability dashboards were standardised.

3.5 Next-Generation Agentic Architectures

The evolution from single-agent to multi-agent systems represents more than incremental improvement—it's a fundamental reimagining of how AI systems collaborate, learn, and scale. By 2025, production deployments have revealed patterns that work and, equally importantly, those that don't.

Multi-Agent Orchestration Patterns:

The theoretical promise of multi-agent systems has crystallised into three dominant architectural patterns; each suited to different use cases and organisational contexts:

1. Hierarchical Orchestration: The Command Structure

In this pattern, a sophisticated "chief-of-staff" agent oversees specialist agents, each handling specific domains. This mirrors traditional organisational structures, making it intuitive for enterprises to adopt.

JPMorgan's loan processing system exemplifies this approach:

- **Orchestrator Agent:** Manages workflow, assigns tasks, synthesises outputs.
- **Credit Analysis Agent:** Evaluates creditworthiness using traditional and alternative data.

- **Fraud Detection Agent:** Screens for suspicious patterns and synthetic identities
- **Document Verification Agent:** Validates income statements, tax returns, and property documents.
- **Compliance Agent:** Ensures adherence to lending regulations and internal policies.
- **Pricing Agent:** Calculates optimal interest rates based on risk and profitability targets.

The orchestrator maintains context across all agents, preventing the inconsistencies that plague disconnected systems. If the fraud agent flags a concern, the orchestrator immediately notifies the credit and pricing agents to adjust their assessments. This coordinated approach reduces loan decision time from days to minutes whilst maintaining—even improving—decision quality.

Implementation considerations:

- Requires sophisticated orchestrator logic to manage dependencies.
- Clear escalation paths for conflicts between specialist agents
- Robust fallback mechanisms when individual agents fail.
- Comprehensive logging for audit and debugging purposes.

2. Collaborative Networks: The Peer Partnership

Rather than hierarchical control, this pattern enables peer agents to negotiate and collaborate dynamically, similar to how human experts might consult on a complex case.

HSBC's trade settlement system demonstrates this approach:

- **Counterparty Validation Agent:** Verifies trading partner credentials and limits.
- **Regulatory Compliance Agent:** Ensures trade meets all jurisdictional requirements.
- **Market Risk Agent:** Assesses exposure and hedging requirements.
- **Settlement Execution Agent:** Manages the actual transfer of securities and funds.
- **Reconciliation Agent:** Matches trades with counterparty records.

These agents communicate through a shared message bus, broadcasting their findings and concerns. When the regulatory agent identifies a restriction, it doesn't wait for permission—it immediately informs all other agents, who adjust their processing accordingly. The agents reach consensus through a voting mechanism when conflicts arise.

Key advantages:

- Resilience through redundancy—no single point of failure
- Faster processing through parallel execution
- Natural load balancing as agents share work.
- Easier to add new agents without restructuring.

Challenges to address:

- Complex debugging when multiple agents interact.
- Potential for circular dependencies or deadlocks
- Need for sophisticated conflict resolution mechanisms
- Higher communication overhead between agents

3. Adaptive Swarms: The Emergent Intelligence

This cutting-edge pattern, still largely experimental in production, allows agents to dynamically form and dissolve teams based on task requirements. Think of it as a "gig economy" for AI agents.

A next-generation customer service implementation might work as follows:

- Customer query arrives with unknown complexity.
- Scout agents quickly assess the query's nature and requirements.
- Relevant specialist agents are dynamically recruited.
- Agents form a temporary team to resolve the issue.
- Team dissolves after resolution, with agents available for other tasks

Early implementations show promise for crisis management scenarios where requirements shift rapidly. During a market flash crash, for instance, swarms can quickly form to handle position management, client communications, regulatory reporting, and liquidity provision—then seamlessly reconfigure as the situation evolves.

Emerging benefits:

- Optimal resource utilisation—agents only engaged when needed.
- Natural scaling with demand
- Adaptation to novel situations without reconfiguration
- Potential for emergent problem-solving strategies

Current limitations:

- Requires sophisticated agent discovery mechanisms.
- Complex orchestration overhead
- Difficult to predict behaviour and performance.
- Regulatory concerns about accountability and control

Memory Architecture Evolution:

Modern agentic systems have moved beyond simple context windows to implement sophisticated memory systems that enable learning, adaptation, and consistency across interactions. Banks implementing these systems report 40% improvements in customer satisfaction due to better continuity and personalisation.

Three-Tier Memory Architecture:

Working Memory (The Active Context):

- Holds current transaction details, conversation history, and immediate goals.
- Typically limited to 32K-128K tokens depending on model capabilities
- Refreshed with each interaction but maintains session continuity.
- Includes attention mechanisms to prioritise relevant information.

Implementation example: A wealth advisory agent maintains the current meeting context, recent portfolio changes, and immediate client concerns. This enables natural conversation flow without repetition.

Episodic Memory (The Experience Bank):

- Stores specific interactions, decisions, and outcomes.
- Indexed by multiple dimensions: time, client, transaction type, outcome.
- Enables learning from past successes and failures.
- Supports "remember when" queries and pattern recognition.

Implementation example: The system recalls that a specific client always calls before major market events, becoming anxious about volatility. The agent proactively addresses these concerns in future interactions.

Semantic Memory (The Knowledge Base):

- Contains domain knowledge, rules, and learned patterns.
- Continuously updated through supervised and unsupervised learning
- Shared across agents for consistent understanding.
- Includes both explicit rules and implicit patterns.

Implementation example: The system knows that certain transaction patterns indicate potential elder financial abuse, regardless of the specific client or account—knowledge accumulated across millions of interactions.

Advanced Memory Techniques:

Memory Consolidation: Like human memory, agent systems now implement consolidation processes. Short-term interactions are periodically reviewed, with important patterns and lessons extracted into long-term semantic memory. Unimportant details are forgotten to prevent memory bloat.

Selective Attention: Not all information deserves equal weight. Modern systems implement attention mechanisms that prioritise memory formation based on:

- Emotional salience (customer frustration or delight)
- Financial significance (large transactions or losses)
- Regulatory importance (compliance-related interactions)
- Novelty (unusual patterns or requests)

Memory Replay: During quiet periods, agents' "replay" past interactions to reinforce learning and identify missed opportunities. This offline learning significantly improves performance without requiring new training data.

Tool Integration Patterns:

The evolution from simple API calls to sophisticated tool use represents perhaps the most practical advancement in agentic AI. Modern frameworks support hundreds of integrated tools, but successful implementations follow clear patterns.

Tool Authentication and Security:

Every tool interaction requires careful security consideration. Banks implement multi-layered security:

- **Agent Identity:** Each agent has cryptographic credentials, with permissions limited to necessary tools.
- **Request Signing:** All tool calls are digitally signed to prevent tampering.
- **Rate Limiting:** Prevents runaway agents from overwhelming systems.
- **Audit Logging:** Every tool interaction is logged for compliance and debugging.

Tool Discovery and Selection:

Modern agents don't just use predetermined tools—they discover and select appropriate tools dynamically:

Tool Registry Pattern:

Tool: CustomerDataAPI
Description: Retrieves customer profile and transaction history
Required Parameters: customer_id, date_range.
Optional Parameters: account_type, transaction_category
Output Format: JSON with customer details and transaction list.
Usage Cost: $0.01 per call
Latency: 50-200ms
Availability: 99.99% SLA

Agents query this registry to understand available capabilities, selecting tools based on task requirements, cost constraints, and performance needs.

Tool Composition:

Sophisticated agents don't just call individual tools—they compose them into complex workflows:

Example: Loan Origination Workflow

1. **Identity Verification Tool** → Validates customer identity.
2. **Credit Bureau API** → Retrieves credit history.
3. **Income Verification Service** → Confirms employment and income.
4. **Property Valuation API** → Estimates collateral value
5. **Risk Scoring Model** → Calculates overall risk.
6. **Pricing Engine** → Determines interest rate.

7. **Document Generation Tool** → Creates loan agreements.

8. **E-Signature Service** → Facilitates digital signing.

The agent orchestrates these tools, handling failures, retries, and alternative paths when specific tools are unavailable.

Reasoning and Planning Architectures:

The latest advancement in agentic systems is sophisticated reasoning capabilities that go beyond simple chain-of-thought prompting.

Tree-of-Thought Reasoning:

When facing complex decisions, agents now explore multiple reasoning paths simultaneously:

Example: Investment Recommendation

```
Root: Client needs investment advice
├── Branch 1: Conservative approach
│   ├── Government bonds
│   ├── High-grade corporate bonds
│   └── Evaluation: Low risk, low return
├── Branch 2: Balanced approach
│   ├── Mixed equity/bond portfolio
│   ├── Diversified sectors
│   └── Evaluation: Moderate risk, moderate return
└── Branch 3: Growth approach
    ├── Technology stocks
    ├── Emerging markets
    └── Evaluation: High risk, high potential return
```

The agent evaluates all branches, considering client circumstances, market conditions, and regulatory constraints before recommending the optimal path.

Monte Carlo Tree Search for Planning:

For multi-step planning problems, agents use Monte Carlo Tree Search (MCTS) to explore possible action sequences:

1. **Selection:** Choose promising paths based on past success
2. **Expansion:** Explore new possibilities
3. **Simulation:** Project likely outcomes
4. **Backpropagation:** Update path values based on simulated results

This approach has proven particularly effective for complex workflows like corporate restructuring or multi-currency trade execution.

Key Take-Aways

- Generative AI supplies brains: tool gateways and policy engines supply **hands and conscience**—together they enable agentic outcomes.
- Track progress on an organisation-wide **A0–A4 maturity curve**; fund moves that shift high-value decisions up one stage.
- Integration discipline (tool abstractions, policy-as-code, observability) beats model sophistication for ROI and regulator trust.

Next-Step Checklist (C-Suite)

To build a resilient and agent-ready architecture, the C-suite must prioritize layered enablement over isolated model deployment. In the first four weeks, the CIO should map the full technology stack—focusing on Layers 4 through 7—to surface critical infrastructure gaps that limit secure, scalable agent deployment. Next, within six weeks, the Head of Engineering must choose or build a secure tool gateway, ensuring that at least three priority enterprise functions are wrapped with appropriate access and control protocols. By week eight, the Product Squad and Risk team should select one Level 1 (A1) use case and uplift it to Level 2 (A2) maturity by integrating multiple tools and embedding policy YAML, setting a precedent for governance-aligned expansion. Finally, within ten weeks, Data Ops should deploy an observability dashboard connected to the CRO's portal, providing real-time visibility into model behaviour, compliance metrics, and risk posture. Together, these steps lay the foundation for safe, scalable Agentic AI operations.

Priority	Action	Owner	Timeframe
1	Map tech stack layers to current estate; identify gaps in layers 4-7	CIO	4 weeks
2	Choose or build a secure tool gateway; wrap 3 priority functions	Head of Engineering	6 weeks
3	Select one A1 use-case: uplift to A2 by adding multi-tool chain & policy YAML	Product squad + Risk	8 weeks
4	Stand up observability dashboard plugged into CRO portal	Data Ops	10 weeks

So What & Call to Action

In today's AI landscape, generative models alone seldom deliver bottom-line impact; the real leap in performance occurs when you tightly integrate those models with operational tools under a rigorous policy framework—shifting from mere content drafting to fully automated, outcome-driven workflows. By adopting the A0–A4 maturity curve, boards gain a shared playbook to benchmark progress, measure risk, and ensure every step toward autonomy is both deliberate and transparent.

Call to Action (Next 120 Days):

1. Audit Your AI Stack: Map your current capabilities against the seven-layer architecture and allocate funding to shore up gaps—especially in your agent orchestrator, tool gateway, and policy engine.

2. Embed the Maturity Curve: Make A0–A4 adoption a board-level metric and require a quarterly heat-map report that visualizes autonomy maturity alongside key risk indicators.

3. Accelerate a Pilot: Select one existing A1 project and fast-track it to A3 using a proven integration playbook; then showcase the results across the organization to ignite momentum.

4. Institutionalize Observability: Elevate your CRO's dashboard to the single source of truth for agent health, performance, and compliance metrics—ensuring real-time visibility and swift corrective action.

By following these steps, you'll transform standalone LLM demos into robust agentic platforms that consistently compound economic value, earn regulator confidence, and liberate your top talent to architect the next generation of digital products.

CHAPTER 4 – Leaders in Action: How Global Banks Deploy Agentic AI

Opening Reflection

When the history of banking's AI transformation is written, 2024-2025 will mark the inflection point where ambition became execution. The leaders profiled in this chapter aren't perfect—they've made mistakes, faced setbacks, and pivoted strategies. But they've done what matters most: moved from PowerPoint to production, from pilots to platforms, from promise to performance. Their journeys offer both inspiration and instruction for institutions at any stage of the agentic journey.

4.1 JPMorgan Chase: The Full-Stack Pioneer

JPMorgan Chase is undergoing what executives describe as a "fundamental rewiring" for the AI era. Their vision extends beyond automation to complete transformation: every employee equipped with AI agents, every back-office process automated, and every client interaction enhanced by AI concierges. This isn't marketing rhetoric—it's a $18 billion annual technology investment strategy with clear deliverables and measurable outcomes.

The LLM Suite Platform: Initially launched to 60,000 employees and now available to over 140,000 staff members globally, LLM Suite serves as JPMorgan's proprietary portal for accessing large language models. Rather than developing proprietary models—a costly and risky endeavour—the bank created an intelligent abstraction layer that can tap into models from OpenAI, Anthropic, and other providers. This approach provides flexibility whilst avoiding vendor lock-in.

As Teresa Heitsenrether, their Chief Data and Analytics Officer, explains: "The plan is not to be beholden to any one model provider. We want to move fluidly across models depending on use cases."

The platform isn't just a chatbot interface. Employees use it for complex tasks including:

- Writing and summarising lengthy documents (reducing report creation time by 70%)
- Problem-solving with Excel and data analysis (catching errors human analysts miss)
- Generating ideas for marketing campaigns and product innovations
- Creating code and debugging applications (developers report 40% productivity gains)
- Analysing customer feedback and identifying patterns across millions of interactions

Measurable Impact: The numbers tell a compelling story. The bank's Contract Intelligence (COiN) system processes commercial loan agreements in seconds rather than hours, eliminating 360,000 hours of legal work annually—equivalent to 180 full-time employees. In a demonstration to journalists, their AI platform created a comprehensive investment banking pitch deck in 30 seconds, complete with market analysis, comparable transactions, and valuation ranges—work that previously required a team of junior bankers working through the night.

Customer service transformation has been equally dramatic. AI-powered systems now handle millions of routine enquiries, freeing human agents to focus on complex, high-value interactions. The bank reports that customers using AI-assisted channels show 15% higher satisfaction scores and 25% lower call-back rates, indicating problems are being resolved correctly the first time.

Infrastructure Investment: JPMorgan's commitment goes beyond software. The bank will spend $18 billion on technology in 2025, up from $17 billion in 2024. Critically, they've modernised their infrastructure foundation: 65% of workloads now run on public or private cloud platforms, up from 50% a year ago. When including applications on virtual servers, that number reaches 80%. This cloud transformation wasn't just about cost—it was about creating the elastic compute infrastructure necessary for AI workloads that can spike 100x during peak processing periods.

The bank has also invested heavily in data architecture. Managing 500 petabytes of data requires industrial-scale systems. They've implemented a modern data lakehouse architecture combining structured and unstructured data, with sophisticated lineage tracking ensuring they can trace any AI decision back to its source data—crucial for regulatory compliance.

Organisational Transformation: Technology alone doesn't drive change—people do. JPMorgan has restructured entire departments around AI capabilities. They've created an AI Centre of Excellence with over 200 data scientists and ML engineers, but more importantly, they've embedded AI expertise within business units. Every major department now has dedicated "AI Champions" who bridge technical and business domains.

Training has been massive in scale: over 40,000 employees have completed AI literacy programmes, 5,000 have received advanced prompt engineering training, and 500 business analysts have been reskilled as "citizen data scientists" capable of building and deploying simple models without engineering support.

4.2 HSBC: The Global Orchestrator

HSBC's AI journey reflects the unique challenges of a truly global bank operating across 64 countries with vastly different regulatory regimes, customer expectations, and technological maturity levels. Their approach—pragmatic, measured, and strategically focused—offers lessons for any institution grappling with complexity at scale.

Strategic Reorganisation: In October 2024, HSBC announced a fundamental restructuring effective January 2025, creating four focused global businesses: Hong Kong, UK, Corporate and Institutional Banking (CIB), and International Wealth and Premier Banking (IWPB). This wasn't just shuffling organisation charts—it was explicitly designed to accelerate AI deployment by creating clearer accountability and enabling faster decision-making. The new CIB division received a specific mandate to pursue "advanced technologies, specifically digitalisation, computing and generative AI" with dedicated budgets and autonomous decision-making authority.

The Wealth Intelligence Platform: HSBC Private Bank's new AI-driven platform represents a masterclass in augmented advisory services. Unlike robo-advisors that attempt to replace human wealth managers, Wealth Intelligence enhances them. The system analyses thousands of data points—client portfolios, risk preferences, life events, market conditions, regulatory changes, and even news sentiment—to generate personalised investment strategies and talking points for relationship managers.

The results have been striking:

- 12-15% increase in assets under management from AI-recommended strategies
- 5-6x improvement in client conversion rates when AI insights are used in pitches

- 3x increase in portfolio review frequency, strengthening client relationships.

- 42% reduction in time spent on administrative tasks by relationship managers.

Crucially, the system maintains the human relationship at its centre. Clients still interact primarily with their relationship manager, but that manager is now equipped with insights that would have required a team of analysts' weeks to compile. One senior wealth advisor described it as "having a team of 20 analysts working for me 24/7, but with perfect memory of every client interaction we've ever had."

Anti-Money Laundering Revolution: HSBC processes millions of transactions daily across multiple currencies, time zones, and regulatory regimes—a money launderer's paradise if not properly monitored. Their AI-driven AML system represents one of the most sophisticated deployments in global banking. The system employs ensemble machine learning models that analyse transaction patterns, customer behaviours, geographical risks, and even news events in real-time.

The transformation metrics are compelling:

- 45% reduction in false positives (legitimate transactions flagged as suspicious)

- 60% increase in true positive detection (actual suspicious activity identified)

- 70% reduction in investigation time through automated evidence gathering.

- 50% decrease in regulatory findings related to AML controls.

The system's sophistication extends beyond simple pattern matching. It understands context—a sudden large transfer might be suspicious for one customer but routine for another based on historical patterns. It adapts to new money laundering techniques by continuously learning from investigated cases. Most importantly, it provides explainable decisions that satisfy regulatory scrutiny, with each alert accompanied by a clear rationale that investigators can verify.

Engineering Productivity Enhancement: Recognising that AI transformation requires massive software development, HSBC has equipped its 40,000+ technology staff with AI-powered coding assistants. Engineers using GitHub Copilot report being 42.6% faster at completing coding tasks, with fewer bugs and more comprehensive testing. The bank has also developed proprietary coding assistants trained on their specific codebases, architectural patterns, and compliance requirements.

This investment in developer productivity has cascading effects:

- New features ship 30% faster.
- Technical debt is addressed more systematically.
- Security vulnerabilities are caught earlier in development.
- Documentation is completer and more consistent.

4.3 Morgan Stanley: The Advisor Augmenter

Morgan Stanley's approach to AI reflects its position as a premier wealth management firm: technology should enhance, not replace, the human advisor relationship. Their multi-year partnership with OpenAI has produced some of the industry's most sophisticated advisor-support tools.

AI @ Morgan Stanley Assistant Evolution: Launched in September 2023 and continuously enhanced since, the AI @ Morgan Stanley Assistant gives the firm's 16,000 financial advisors instant access to insights from over 100,000 research reports and documents. But this isn't just a search engine—it's a reasoning system that understands context, synthesises information, and provides actionable insights.

An advisor preparing for a client meeting can ask questions like: "What are the tax implications of selling Tesla stock for a California resident who's retiring to Florida next year, and how might upcoming Fed decisions impact the timing?" The system provides comprehensive answers drawing from tax code, state regulations, market analysis, and economic forecasts—work that would have taken hours of research condensed into seconds.

AI @ Morgan Stanley Debrief: Launched in June 2024, this tool revolutionises how advisors capture and utilise meeting insights. Using advanced speech recognition and natural language processing, it:

- Transcribes client meetings (with consent) with 98% accuracy.
- Extracts key decisions, action items, and concerns automatically.
- Updates CRM systems without manual data entry
- Identifies cross-selling opportunities based on conversation analysis.
- Flags compliance issues or regulatory concerns in real-time

Advisors report saving 10 hours weekly on administrative tasks, time now spent on client engagement and business development. More importantly, no crucial detail is lost—every client preference, concern, or goal is captured and accessible for future interactions.

Next Best Action System: Perhaps most impressively, Morgan Stanley's AI analyses vast amounts of data to recommend personalised actions for each client. The system considers:

- Portfolio performance and risk metrics
- Life events (retirement, marriage, inheritance)
- Market conditions and economic indicators
- Regulatory changes affecting the client.
- Historical interaction patterns and preferences

It then suggests specific actions: rebalancing recommendations, tax-loss harvesting opportunities, insurance needs, estate planning updates, or simply a check-in call for clients who haven't been contacted recently. Advisors following AI recommendations see 25% higher client retention and 35% greater asset growth compared to those who don't.

Measurable Business Impact: CEO Ted Pick's recent earnings call revealed the concrete benefits: "The AI @ Morgan Stanley Assistant is just the first chapter of what we're going to do across the financial advisor platform. That's where we think we're going to have some real edge." The numbers support his confidence:

- 20% increase in advisor productivity
- 30% reduction in compliance violations
- 15% improvement in client satisfaction scores
- $50 billion in additional assets under management attributed to AI-driven insights.

4.4 Bank of America: The Scale Player

Summary:

- Bank of America's Erica evolution
- Real progression from 2018 launch to 2 billion interactions by 2025
- Actual NPS improvements and customer metrics
- Concrete ROI: $500 million annual savings

Bank of America's AI strategy emphasises scale and standardisation across its massive retail footprint: 66 million consumer and small business clients, 3,900 financial centres, and 15,000 ATMs. Their approach proves that AI transformation isn't just for boutique operations—it can work at massive scale.

Erica: The Virtual Financial Assistant Launched in 2018 and continuously enhanced, Erica has become one of banking's most successful AI deployments. By 2025, Erica has handled over 2 billion client interactions, with 50 million clients using the service regularly. But Erica has evolved far beyond simple balance enquiries:

- **Predictive Insights:** Analyses spending patterns to warn clients before they overdraft.
- **Subscription Management:** Identifies forgotten recurring charges and helps cancel them.
- **Financial Coaching:** Provides personalised budgeting advice based on spending habits.

- **Proactive Alerts:** Notifies clients of unusual charges, fee-avoidance opportunities, and bill due dates.
- **Investment Guidance:** Offers basic investment education and connects to human advisors for complex needs.

The sophistication shows in the numbers: clients using Erica have 15% higher deposit balances, 20% lower overdraft fees, and 25% higher digital engagement rates. The virtual assistant handles 90% of queries without human intervention, saving an estimated $500 million annually in customer service costs.

CashPro Chat for Corporate Clients: Whilst Erica serves retail clients, CashPro Chat supports corporate treasurers managing complex cash positions. The AI assistant can:

- Answer questions about payment status across multiple countries.
- Provide real-time foreign exchange rates and execution.
- Generate custom reports on cash positions.
- Alert treasurers to potential liquidity issues.
- Facilitate wire transfers with natural language commands.

Corporate clients using CashPro Chat report 40% reduction in time spent on routine treasury tasks and 60% faster problem resolution.

4.5 Lessons from the Leaders

Analysing these implementations reveals consistent patterns that separate success from failure:

1. Platform Over Point Solutions: Every successful bank built a platform approach rather than deploying disconnected AI tools. JPMorgan's LLM Suite, HSBC's integrated architecture, and Morgan Stanley's advisor platform all provide consistent experiences across use cases.

2. Human-Centric Design: None of these banks attempted to replace human's wholesale. Instead, they augmented human capabilities, freeing workers from mundane tasks to focus on relationship building and complex problem-solving.

3. Measurement Obsession: Each institution established clear metrics before deployment and measured relentlessly. They know precisely what AI contributes to their bottom line.

4. Governance First: Rather than treating compliance as an afterthought, these banks embedded governance into their AI platforms from day one. Policy-as-code, audit trails, and explainability were design requirements, not additions.

5. Continuous Evolution: These aren't static deployments. Each bank continuously enhances their AI capabilities, learning from usage patterns and user feedback to improve functionality.

CHAPTER 5 – Customer Obsession & Ecosystems: Building the Data-Network Flywheel

In a near future, business review headline will read: (the following statement is purely illustrative, and the person and Bank cited are fictional)

"Our best-selling product last quarter didn't exist six months ago. A partner launched it on our platform using three APIs and 30 lines of code."
— **Sofia Alvarez, Chief Digital Officer, NuevaBank**

Financial services used to win on balance-sheet strength or branch footprint. Today the durable moat is a **data-network effect**: every customer interaction generates proprietary data that improves the next interaction, attracting more customers and partners, creating yet more data. This virtuous flywheel spins fastest inside an open—but well-governed—ecosystem of APIs, fintech partners, and digital channels. This chapter shows how customer obsession translates into ecosystem strategy, the metrics boards should track, and the pitfalls that stall network effects.

Opening Vignette – The 90-Second Mortgage

São Paulo, July 2025. A ride-share driver taps a button in her gig-work app: *"Pre-qualify for home loan."* Behind the scenes, the app calls **NuevaBank's** open-credit API, streams income data, and receives an agentic underwriting decision in 12 seconds. E-sign follows, registry filing completes, and funds hit the seller—all in 90 seconds. The driver shares the experience on social media; within 48 hours, 8 000 more gig workers apply. Application data trains NuevaBank's risk models, shrinking error bands, lowering pricing, and pulling still more volume. The flywheel turns.

5.1 Why Customer Obsession Demands an Ecosystem

In an age where customers judge every interaction against their very best digital experiences—whether that's a seamless ride-share pickup or an effortless streaming signup—meeting hyper-personalized expectations requires more than isolated point solutions. By embracing an ecosystem strategy, organizations can "borrow" rich contextual insights—like mobility patterns or purchase histories—that they don't own internally, instantly elevating onboarding and service delivery. Moreover, while in-house teams might launch a handful of new features annually, opening your platform to external developers multiplies innovation throughput, with hundreds of creative solutions deployed on your rails. This collaborative model also spreads the risk of experimentation—partner portfolios can trial novel ideas, and if a concept falters, it's gracefully sunset without unsettling your core operations. The key insight is that obsession with outcomes—delivering the right customer experience—far outweighs the need to own every single touchpoint. You retain control of the platform's foundation, but empower a broader network to drive speed, scale, and relevance in ways no single organization could achieve alone.

Key Insight: Obsession with *outcomes* over *ownership* unlocks speed. You own the platform, not every customer touchpoint.

5.2 The Data-Network Flywheel

Building a high-performing Agentic AI system depends on more than just great models—it requires a self-reinforcing data network flywheel. This flywheel starts with Acquire: reduce the "Time to First

Yes" (TtFY)—how fast a user receives value from their first interaction. Dropping TtFY below 5 minutes correlates with 3–5x faster active user growth, according to BCG's 2025 Fintech Benchmark. Next is Engage—does system usage increase the quality of each interaction? Track KPIs like session NPS and feature adoption rate. Then comes Enrich: are you capturing proprietary data signals that deepen the learning loop? Daily unique data points (DUDP) become the key currency here. In the Adapt stage, assess whether models are learning quickly and redeploying themselves in real-time—measured by model refresh cadence. Finally, attract external builders—are partners using your APIs to create new value? Monthly Active Partners (MAP) and gross merchandise value (GMV) via those partners are powerful signals of flywheel maturity. Each stage compounds the next, creating exponential value—if designed with intentional metrics and velocity in mind.

Flywheel Stage	Questions to Ask	Example KPI
Acquire	Do we reduce time-to-value for first transaction?	Time-to-first-yes (TtFY)
Engage	Does interaction quality improve with usage?	Session NPS, feature adoption rate
Enrich	Are we capturing proprietary signals each cycle?	Daily unique data points (DUDP)
Adapt	Do models learn fast and deploy automatically?	Model refresh cadence
Attract	Are partners building atop our APIs?	Monthly active partners (MAP), GMV via partners

Firms that reduce **TtFY** below 5 minutes grow active user bases 3-5× faster than peers, according to BCG's 2025 Fintech Benchmark.

5.3 Ecosystem Archetypes & Monetisation Models

Across the evolving landscape of financial services, four strategic archetypes have emerged as the linchpins of platform-driven growth. First is the Distribution Hub, which leverages a bank's customer base to funnel high-value referrals to fintech partners—think the Apple Card powered by Goldman Sachs—monetizing through referral fees and revenue share. Next, the Capability Marketplace transforms core banking functions into modular APIs, enabling ventures like Stripe Treasury to embed deposit, lending, and payment services directly into third-party applications, with usage-based pricing unlocking new revenue streams. The Data Utility model turns proprietary transaction and behavioural insights into subscription offerings—such as Visa Spend Insights—letting banks monetize anonymized data sets while empowering partners with actionable analytics. Finally, the Orchestration Platform stitches together multi-partner journeys on a single interface, exemplified by WeChat Pay's mini-program ecosystem, where take-rates on transaction flows crystallize the platform's value. Together, these archetypes illustrate how banks can evolve from siloed product providers into dynamic ecosystems, each leveraging distinct value propositions and monetization levers to thrive in the digital age.

Archetype	Value Proposition	Monetisation	Famous Example
Distribution Hub	Provide customers to fintechs	Referral fees, rev-share	Apple Card via Goldman Sachs
Capability Marketplace	Offer bank services via APIs	Usage-based pricing	Stripe Treasury with banks
Data Utility	Monetise proprietary data sets	Insights subscription	Visa *Spend Insights*
Orchestration Platform	Coordinate multi-partner journeys	Take-rate on flow	WeChat Pay mini-programs

Banks often evolve through these archetypes sequentially starting with distribution partnerships and maturing into orchestration roles once policy-as-code and settlement rails are battle-tested.

5.4 Integration Patterns that Scale

1. In architecting a scalable, partner-centric platform, start by designing a **thin API layer** that exposes only essential functions, and push all governance logic into a **thick policy engine** so that every partner integration inherits your risk controls by default. Embrace **event-driven design**: broadcast customer consent and transaction events in real time, letting partners subscribe on demand rather than resorting to inefficient polling. Ensure consistency and security with a unified **sandbox-to-production pipeline**, so both internal teams and external developers follow the same CI/CD path with identical security gates. Make **telemetry a first-class citizen**: stream anonymized call metrics from every external interaction into your analytics lake—because what you can't measure, you can't improve.

2. Consider GrabFin'[10]s Singapore rollout as a blueprint: by exposing loan, insurance, and card APIs to ride-hail merchants through a rigorously enforced sandbox pipeline, they doubled their financial-services revenue within a year and drove a 180 percent increase in monthly active partner growth. This combination of lean interfaces, embedded governance, real-time events, and relentless measurement turned a simple API strategy into a powerhouse ecosystem.

10 https://fintechnews.my/31490/e-wallets-malaysia/grab-financial-group-unveils-its-new-brand-grabfin/

5.5 Governing the Ecosystem without Killing It

For each critical risk domain, we've established a corresponding governance mechanism and designated ownership to ensure accountability and control. To prevent customer data misuse, we enforce OAuth 2.0 scopes combined with a comprehensive consent ledger, overseen by the Chief Privacy Officer. To guard against model bias, every partner-supplied algorithm must pass a mandatory bias-testing protocol under the supervision of the AI Risk Lead. For liquidity and settlement risks, real-time limit checks are implemented through our policy engine, with the Treasury CRO holding responsibility. Finally, to manage brand and conduct exposures, we maintain an ongoing partner scorecard and a kill-switch API, both managed by the Chief Brand Officer, ensuring we can swiftly intervene if standards slip.

Risk Domain	Guard-Rail Mechanism	Ownership
Customer Data Misuse	OAuth 2.0 scopes, consent ledger	Chief Privacy Officer
Model Bias	Mandatory bias test on partner-supplied models	AI Risk Lead
Liquidity & Settlement	Real-time limit checks via policy engine	Treasury CRO
Brand & Conduct	Partner scorecard; kill-switch API	Chief Brand Officer

Successful platforms bake guard-rails into code. Manual partner reviews won't scale when you court thousands of developers.

Key Take-Aways

- In today's platform economy, speed matters more than an exhaustive feature set: by minimizing integration friction, you empower partners to build out the long tail of capabilities, turning your ecosystem into a self-service innovation engine.

- As each interaction feeds back into your data fabric, network effects compound—every transaction, consent event, or API call sharpens your insights and strengthens the moat around your business in a way that competitors without your depth of data simply cannot replicate.

- Underpinning it all is the principle of "governance as code": embedding policy directly into your infrastructure not only gives partners the freedom to innovate at pace, but also assures customers and regulators that safety, compliance, and accountability are baked in from day one.

Next-Step Checklist (C-Suite)

Over the next twelve weeks, your leadership team will execute a tightly scoped, time-bound roadmap designed to accelerate developer onboarding, expand core API offerings, embed robust consent and compliance controls, and establish real-time observability—all under clear ownership. By defining a sub-five-minute "Time to First Yes" target, exposing high-demand APIs, implementing a consent ledger with a kill switch, and launching a telemetry-driven sandbox, you'll drastically reduce friction, strengthen governance, and build momentum for sustained ecosystem growth.

Strategic Actions in One Paragraph

In Week 1–4, the Chief Customer Officer will codify a north-star **Time to First Yes** target of under five minutes—mirroring best practices in API programs that have improved Time to First Call by 20×[11] through streamlined collections and executable request formats. From Weeks 1–8, the CIO and Product teams will unlock three high-demand services—KYC, payments, and credit—by exposing APIs designed for seamless integration and AML compliance, as demonstrated by leading KYC-as-a-service[12] offerings. By Week 10, the CPO and Risk leaders will deploy an **OAuth-based consent ledger**[13] and partner kill-switch—leveraging open-source consent ledger platforms that ensure continuous policy evolution and regulatory alignment. Finally, in Weeks 1–12, the Head of DevX will stand up a developer sandbox instrumented with **OpenTelemetry** hooks—following Kubernetes sandbox design patterns and best practices for real-time streaming of anonymized latency, drift, and fairness metrics to your CRO dashboard.

Priority	Action	Owner	Timeframe
1	Define a north-star **Time-to-First-Yes** target (<5 min)	Chief Customer Officer	4 weeks
2	Expose three high-demand APIs (KYC, payments, credit)	CIO + Product	8 weeks
3	Implement consent ledger + kill-switch for partners	CPO + Risk	10 weeks
4	Launch developer sandbox with telemetry hooks	Head of DevX	12 weeks

11 https://blog.postman.com/improve-your-time-to-first-api-call-by-20x/

12 https://usesmileid.com/blog/kyc-api/

13 https://www.pwc.in/assets/pdfs/consulting/technology/data-and-analytics/govern-your-data/insights/a-blueprint-for-robust-consent-management.pdf

So What & Call to Action

Over the next 120 days, four focused initiatives—setting a sub-five-minute "Time to First Yes" goal, exposing a core API bundle with built-in consent and kill-switch controls, deploying comprehensive API telemetry, and standing up a dedicated developer relations squad—will radically accelerate your transition from siloed product teams to a dynamic, self-reinforcing ecosystem. By marrying speed with governance and developer-centricity, you'll not only reduce friction and time-to-value, but also build the credibility, data-network effects, and partner momentum that power sustained growth.

Why These Steps Matter

1. Speed Drives Adoption

A shortened "Time to First Yes" is more than a vanity metric—it directly correlates with increased API uptake and partner satisfaction. Postman found that removing onboarding hurdles can improve Time to First Call by up to 20×, driving faster integration and earlier value recognition.

2. Governance Unlocks Scale

Embedding consent ledgers and kill-switch controls within your API bundle ensures every external integration inherits your risk framework by default. NCHL's cross-border API specifications demonstrate how built-in consent management is critical for AML/CFT compliance, while KYC Hub[14] emphasizes that robust API compliance underpins trust with customers and regulators alike.

14 https://www.kychub.com/blog/api-compliance/

3. Observability Transforms Management

Streaming latency, error rates, and adoption metrics from day one gives you the real-time visibility needed to enforce SLAs, spot regressions, and iterate rapidly. Moesif[15] ranks API metrics—especially route-level latency breakdowns—as indispensable for diagnosing performance issues before they impact end users.

4. Developer Relations Fuels Innovation

Treating third-party builders as premium customers creates a virtuous cycle of feedback and advocacy. Google's Developer Relations model—complete with global events, detailed documentation, and open-source contributions—illustrates how strategic DevRel[16] engagement drives product visibility and user adoption.

The Transformative Impact

Commit to these four steps, and you will convert proof-of-concept demos into a fully operational, agentic platform that compounds economic value and wins regulatory trust. A five-minute onboarding target becomes your north star for agility; a lovable API bundle becomes the engine for ecosystem expansion; telemetry dashboards become your single source of truth for operational health; and a developer relations squad becomes the catalyst for a thriving community of innovators. Together, these actions don't just improve processes—they turn customer obsession into a self-reinforcing growth engine that scales.

---

15 https://www.moesif.com/blog/technical/api-metrics/API-Metrics-That-Every-Platform-Team-Should-be-Tracking/

16 https://dev.to/danizeres/how-to-build-a-great-developer-relations-strategy-449a

CHAPTER 6 – Sector Playbooks: Lending, Insurance & Wealth

Here we spotlight how three distinct lines of business—lending, insurance, and wealth—each leverage the same foundational AI engine but extract value in sector-specific ways.

In a near future, business review headline will read: (the following statement is purely illustrative, and the person and Bank cited are fictional)

"We deployed one lending agent every Friday—within a quarter our approval rate jumped 24 pp while defaults fell," recalls **Rajiv Patel, Head of SME Credit** at **AxisOne Bank**.

Across the lending sector, AI-driven underwriting has accelerated decision cycles from days to minutes, boosting approval rates by up to 25 pp[17] and cutting default rates by as much as 15 percent through real-time predictive analytics. This surge in cycle-time agility and risk precision underpins lending's modern playbook[18], where limit adjustments occur in the moment rather than the quarter.

In insurance, the battleground shifts to speed of settlement and micro-priced risk pools. Parametric[19] claims platforms now trigger automated payouts in under thirty minutes by ingesting high-frequency weather and IoT data, slashing adjuster costs by up to 70

17 https://gitnux.org/ai-in-the-consumer-lending-industry-statistics/

18 https://sapidblue.com/insights/read-how-ai-reduces-loan-defaults-with-predictive-analytics/

19 https://www.forbes.com/sites/ruthfoxeblader/2024/02/15/ai-is-supercharging-parametric-insurance/

percent. These weather-data agents enable insurers to offer transparent, fixed-trigger policies that free capital and deepen customer trust—transforming claims from a reactive slog into a proactive service experience.

Wealth management's frontier lies in ultra-personalized portfolios and tax-efficient architectures. Robo-advisor[20] platforms customize allocations to individual goals—whether retirement, education, or income generation—while automated tax-loss harvesting algorithms reduce capital gains taxes by up to 30 percent. Firms like Betterment and Wealthfront deploy AI to reoptimize portfolios daily, melding behavioural finance insights with low-cost ETFs to deliver both performance and fiscal prudence.

What unites these sector playbooks is a shared backbone—robust data fabrics, pretrained foundation models, policy-as-code guardrails, and decision orchestrators—but nuanced agent configurations tailored to each domain's KPI: cycle-time delta for lending, payout velocity for insurance, and after-tax return for wealth. In the pages ahead, we'll unpack the high-value decision points that deserve priority, the agent archetypes proven to move the needle, and the board-level metrics—like ROE uplift, NPS improvement, and regulatory compliance scores—that keep each playbook on track. By understanding how leading institutions calibrate their AI engines to sector-specific goals, you'll gain a blueprint for deploying agents that deliver rapid, measurable impact in your own business lines.

20 https://www.financedispatch.com/what-is-robo-advisory-and-how-does-it-assist-in-personalized-investment-strategies/

Opening Vignette – Three Sectors, Three Surges

- In an instant, the same agentic architecture delivers game-changing results across lending, insurance, and wealth management. In Sydney, a mortgage-approval agent slashes turnaround from 48 hours to just four minutes by seamlessly chaining bureau data, e-signatures, and land-registry APIs within strict policy guardrails. Half a world away in Jakarta, a parametric flood-insurance agent taps satellite rain-rate and river-sensor feeds to trigger payouts before the river even crests—cutting adjuster costs by 70 percent. Meanwhile in New York, a robo-portfolio agent rebalances ETFs at 2 a.m. when China unexpectedly cuts rates, capturing USD 3 million in overnight alpha while client's sleep.

- These "three surges" underscore a simple truth: whether accelerating credit, automating claims, or harvesting market opportunities, it's the same layered engine—data fabric, foundation models, domain adaptors, decision orchestrators, and secure action gateways—tuned to sector-specific levers that drives transformative value. In the chapters ahead, we'll explore how each line of business tailors that engine to its unique KPIs—from agility and risk precision in lending, to instantaneous payouts in insurance, to hyper-personalized, tax-efficient portfolios in wealth. By spotlighting the high-impact decisions, agent patterns, and board-level metrics that matter most, this playbook will equip you to deploy and govern your own agents for rapid, measurable impact.

6.1 High-Value Decision Map by Sector

Across banking's core verticals, autonomous agents are poised to transform critical decision points and drive measurable performance gains. In **lending**, agents can underwrite new applications, optimize credit limits, adjust pricing dynamically, and sequence collections—boosting net interest margins, reducing charge-off rates, and lifting overall ROE. In **insurance**, automated systems excel at granular risk pricing, first-notice-of-loss triage, fraud detection, and instant claims payouts, which together shrink loss and combined ratios while enhancing NPS. And in **wealth management**, robo-advisors rebalance portfolios, execute tax-loss harvesting, screen for ESG alignment, and trigger liquidity alerts—fuelling AUM growth, lowering client churn, and increasing fee yield. By targeting these high-impact use cases, financial institutions can deploy agentic platforms that not only streamline operations but also amplify the metrics that matter most to executives and shareholders.

Sector	Decisions Ripe for Agents	Impact KPI
Lending	Underwrite, limit management, dynamic pricing, collections sequencing	Net interest margin, charge-off rate, ROE
Insurance	Risk pricing, FNOL triage, fraud flagging, claims payout	Loss ratio, combined ratio, NPS
Wealth	Portfolios rebalance, tax-loss harvesting, ESG screening, liquidity alerts	AUM growth, churn rate, fee yield

Tip: Target decisions that swing ≥ $1 million P&L per year or touch customer anxiety points.

6.2 Agent Patterns That Work

Across the financial services landscape, three agentic patterns have emerged as reliable workhorses—each tailored to a specific line of business yet unified by a shared architecture of sensing, reasoning, acting, and governance—delivering transformative speed and precision. In lending, the "Credit Inline" pattern brings underwriting directly into the flow of customer interaction: agents continuously sense income streams and bureau data, ingesting real-time salary credits, transaction histories, and credit scores to build a holistic risk picture. They then reason against loan-to-value thresholds, fraud detection models, and affordability rules, applying conditional logic to assess whether a new application should be approved, what limit to assign, and at what pricing tier. Acting on that insight, the agent issues a dynamic approval or counter-offer in under five minutes—seamlessly integrating with origination systems and notification channels—while governance is enforced through policy-as-code in declarative YAML files that codify maximum exposure limits, fairness constraints, and escalation paths if thresholds are breached. The result is a dramatic compression of decision cycle time—shrinking what once took days into a sub-five-minute interaction—while preserving control and compliance through a well-defined guardrail framework. In insurance, the "Parametric Payout" pattern leverages automatically sourced IoT and satellite feeds—precipitation levels, river gauge readings, and seismic activity metrics—to sense environmental triggers against covered perils. The reasoning layer encodes precise coverage trigger logic, translating raw sensor data into binary decisions: if rainfall exceeds a preset millimeter threshold or groundwater levels surpass a flood risk level, the agent proceeds to the next step. Acting through a smart contract on a distributed ledger, the agent executes an automatic payout directly to policyholders' accounts—bypassing manual claims adjusters and contracting counterparties—while the policy engine logs every transaction in a tamper-evident claims ledger and updates a regulator-facing portal in real time. By automating first notice of loss, fraud checks, and payment execution, parametric agents can settle valid claims in under thirty minutes, slashing adjuster costs by 70 percent and enhancing customer satisfaction through instant relief. Meanwhile, in wealth management, the "Portfolio Swarm" pattern enlists an ensemble of specialized agents to optimize clients' holdings around the clock: front-line agents sense live market tick data and continuous updates to each client's risk profile, blending price movements, volatility indices, and portfolio drift alerts. The reasoning layer comprises multiple agents, each responsible for a discrete asset bucket—equities, fixed income, alternatives—applying optimization algorithms to determine target weights, rebalancing thresholds, and tax-loss harvesting opportunities. These agents act swiftly via trade APIs, executing buy or sell orders, reallocating tax lots, and reinvesting proceeds according to predefined constraints. Governance is embedded through drift-limit policies and wash-sale guards that prevent regulatory breaches and ensure tax-efficient implementation. With rebalance latency measured in seconds—often below sixty seconds from signal to execution—the swarm pattern preserves portfolio alignment and captures fleeting market inefficiencies, contributing to sustained AUM growth and improved client retention. Taken together, these agent patterns underscore a fundamental truth: while the core AI engine—data fabric, foundational models, and policy orchestration—remains consistent across use cases, the true business impact lies in selecting and fine-tuning the specific sensing inputs, reasoning frameworks, action capabilities, and governance guardrails that align to each sector's priorities. Whether compressing credit cycle times, delivering instant insurance relief, or optimizing wealth portfolios in real time, these patterns translate complex workflows into autonomous, policy-governed processes that deliver measurable KPIs: net interest margin and ROE uplift in lending, loss ratio and NPS improvement in insurance, and AUM growth plus fee yield enhancements in wealth. By codifying these blueprints, institutions can replicate success across business lines, scaling their AI investments with confidence and driving operational excellence at unprecedented speed.

6.3 Integration & Governance Nuances

Across financial sectors, the integration and governance requirements vary significantly but follow a shared principle of embedding controls close to the point of action, needless to say that agents should have ethics framework embedded. In lending, systems must interface with land-registry services (e.g., HM Land Registry APIs) and e-signature platforms to verify property titles and capture legally binding consents before credit is extended. The primary governance hotspot here is fair-lending bias and credit-line caps, which demand policy-as-code guardrails to ensure automated decisions comply with regulatory fairness mandates and exposure limits.

In insurance, agents rely on real-time hazard feeds—such as IoT sensors and satellite-derived catastrophe data—to trigger claims automatically when preset conditions are met, exemplified by Moody's Location Risk Intelligence API[21] for instant risk screening. Oversight centers on regulatory solvency limits, requiring continuous monitoring of capital adequacy under frameworks like Solvency II[22] or the NAIC's risk-based capital standards to guarantee insurers remain solvent after automated payouts.

For wealth management, platforms must integrate across multiple execution venues—equities, fixed income, and alternatives—via order and execution management systems to achieve best-execution outcomes. Governance hotspots include best-execution evidence under SEC rules and tax compliance, where wash-sale and tax-lot management rules must be encoded to avoid prohibited trading patterns and ensure fiduciary duty. By aligning each domain's unique integration needs with tailored policy engines, institutions can automate complex workflows securely and in full regulatory compliance.

21 https://www.moodys.com/web/en/us/who-we-serve/insurance/intelligent-risk-platform/location-intelligence.html

22 https://www.soa.org/sections/education-research/educ-research-newsletter/2021/august/ehn-2021-08-wang/

Domain	Unique Integration Need	Governance Hot-Spot
Lending	Land-registry & e-sign APIs	Fair-lending bias, credit-line caps
Insurance	Real-time hazard data	Regulatory solvency limits
Wealth	Multi-asset execution venues	Best-execution evidence, tax rules

Key Take-Aways

Across finance's major verticals, a single AI[23] "engine"—comprised of layered data fabrics, foundational models, and policy orchestration—can be fine-tuned with sector-specific triggers and guardrails to drive outsized value in lending, insurance, and wealth management. Shrinking cycle times not only accelerates decision throughput but also underpins both margin expansion and customer loyalty, as firms that cut loan or claim turnaround from days to minutes see double-digit improvements in key performance metrics[24]. Yet adoption hinges on embedding governance[25] at the heart of every workflow—regulators prioritize fairness and anti-bias in lending, solvency and capital adequacy in insurance, and best-execution evidence in wealth management.

- **One engine, many levers.** A unified AI architecture serves as the backbone for diverse use cases, but true differentiation comes from tailoring sensing triggers, reasoning frameworks,

23 https://www.ey.com/en_gr/insights/financial-services/how-artificial-intelligence-is-reshaping-the-financial-services-industry

24 https://www.mckinsey.com/industries/financial-services/our-insights/scaling-gen-ai-in-banking-choosing-the-best-operating-model

25 https://www.weforum.org/stories/2024/12/agentic-ai-financial-services-autonomy-efficiency-and-inclusion/

and policy guardrails to each sector's unique economics. This approach amplifies efficiency while preserving control, as leading institutions demonstrate by combining consistent infrastructure with specialized agent patterns[26].

- **Cycle time is gold.** Every minute shaved off credit underwriting or claims settlement translates into improved net interest margins, reduced loss ratios, and higher customer satisfaction. McKinsey[27] research shows that organizations reducing decision latency by over 80 percent unlock productivity gains worth up to 4.7 percent of total revenues.

- **Governance shapes adoption.** Embedding[28] "policy as code" ensures automated processes meet regulatory expectations: fairness mandates in consumer lending, solvency and reserve requirements in insurance, and best-execution and tax compliance in wealth. Firms excelling in this embedding see faster board approval, higher audit confidence, and stronger regulatory partnerships.

Next-Step Checklist (C-Suite)

Over the next three months, your executive team will execute four pivotal initiatives to transition from pilot projects to enterprise-wide agentic operations. First, within four weeks, each line-of-business head must identify and map the top ten high-value decisions in their sector, creating a clear blueprint for automation prioritization. By Week 8, the Product and Risk teams will collaborate to build and benchmark a reference agent in each domain—measuring cycle-time

26 https://www.ey.com/en_gr/insights/financial-services/how-artificial-intelligence-is-reshaping-the-financial-services-industry

27 https://www.mckinsey.com/industries/financial-services/our-insights/scaling-gen-ai-in-banking-choosing-the-best-operating-model

28 https://www.forbes.com/councils/forbesfinancecouncil/2023/12/26/the-benefits-and-risks-of-ai-in-financial-services/

improvements and error rates against defined targets. In Week 10, the AI Risk Lead will codify those learnings into sector-specific policy YAML templates, ensuring every automated decision inherits robust governance from day one. Finally, by the 12-week mark, the CIO's office will convene a cross-sector "Agent Guild" to share best practices, reuse proven patterns, and drive continuous improvement across all business lines.

Priority	Action	Owner	Timeframe
1	Map top-10 high-value decisions per sector line	Line of Business Heads	4 weeks
2	Build one reference agent for each sector: benchmark cycle-time & error-rate	Product + Risk	8 weeks
3	Publish sector-specific policy YAML templates	AI Risk Lead	10 weeks
4	Stand-up cross-sector "Agent Guild" to reuse patterns	CIO Office	12 weeks

So What & Call to Action

So what?

Agentic AI delivers exceptional returns when it addresses the precise pain points unique to each line of business. In lending, real-time underwriting accelerates credit decisions and expands margins; in insurance, automated parametric payouts transform claims into instant customer delight; in wealth management, continuous, intelligent rebalancing captures market opportunities around the clock. A one-size-fits-all approach overlooks these nuances—and in doing so, forfeits both profit and hard-won customer trust.

Call to Action (Next 120 Days)

1. Zero in on Your Killer Use Case: Identify the single highest-value decision in lending, insurance, and wealth. Secure funding for an agent prototype, then tie its success directly to a P&L metric—whether that's net interest margin, loss ratio reduction, or incremental AUM growth.

2. Embed Guardrails from Day One: Translate compliance and risk boundaries into policy-as-code. For lending, integrate mandatory bias-testing workflows; for insurance, codify capital adequacy caps; for wealth, automate best-execution attestations. By baking these controls into your YAML templates, you ensure safe experimentation without slowing innovation.

3. Measure Cycle Time Relentlessly: Track end-to-end decision latency before and after deployment. Expose these metrics on a shared dashboard, celebrate double-digit improvements, and use the data to optimize your agent's reasoning and action loops.

4. Create an Agent Guild for Cross-Pollination: Establish a forum where sector teams share data-pipeline architectures, policy modules, and observability dashboards. Leveraging proven patterns accelerates each line of business's journey from isolated pilots to a unified, compounding network of intelligent agents.

By focusing on the decisions that move your core metrics, enforcing governance as code, and relentlessly tracking performance, you'll transform standalone experiments into a harmonized fleet of agentic platforms. The result: sustained profitability lifts hand-in-hand with elevated customer satisfaction—and a dynamic, scalable engine for future innovation.

CHAPTER 7 – AI-Driven Payments & Transactions: Real-Time Rails, Fraud Prediction, DeFi & CBDCs

In a near future, business review headline will read: (the following statement is purely illustrative, and the person and Bank cited are fictional)

"The payment rail is now an API market—agents negotiate fees and FX in milliseconds." — **Helena Ng, Global Head of Payments, Triton Bank**

Margin on traditional payments is collapsing while customer tolerance for latency rounds down to *zero*. The winners orchestrate **agents** that route flows, predict fraud, optimise liquidity, and even swap into stablecoins or wholesale CBDCs when fiat rails sleep. This chapter maps the rail landscape, the agent patterns that matter, and the guard-rails that keep regulators calm.

Opening Vignette – The Invisible Checkout

In today's borderless digital economy, a single "Pay Now" tap can trigger a symphony of invisible, real-time financial operations—what we call the Invisible Checkout. Picture a gamer in Buenos Aires snapping up limited-edition sneakers from a Seoul e-commerce site. The moment they confirm the purchase; three autonomous agents kick into gear:

First, an **FX routing agent** assesses available rails—FedNow's instant-payment network in the U.S., Brazil's PIX system, and Ethereum Layer 2 solutions—analyzing fees, settlement speed, and counterparty risk. Within milliseconds, it selects the optimal path that minimizes both cost and latency, ensuring the gamer pays the best possible rate.

Next, a **fraud-vector agent** springs into action. It stitches together "device DNA" (everything from browser fingerprint to OS version), geolocation data, and behavior embeddings derived from the gamer's historical transaction patterns. In just **310 ms**, it clears the transaction, flagging nothing suspicious and granting instant approval.

Meanwhile, a **treasury agent** hedges the Argentine peso–Korean won exposure via a DeFi swap—choosing between decentralized exchange pools—and then automatically sweeps any surplus won into a money-market smart contract to earn yield until disbursement requirements arise. This decentralized approach ensures capital efficiency and embeds real-time liquidity management without manual intervention.

By the time the sneaker image appears in the gamer's order history, the merchant has already received settlement on a T+0 basis, and the bank has booked its FX spread margin—all without a single human keystroke. For the user, it's as simple as a green check mark. Behind the scenes, however, this secure choreography of agents is redefining trust and efficiency in cross-border payments: faster, cheaper, and more seamless than ever before—truly, the future of checkout is invisible.

7.1 Rail Landscape Snapshot (2025)

As we step into 2025, the global payments "rail" landscape is defined by near-instantaneous settlement speeds and rapid volume growth, each network offering distinct opportunities for AI-driven optimization. In the United States, FedNow's sub-15-second finality has set a new benchmark for instant domestic transfers, presenting fertile ground for smart-routing agents that can dynamically choose the most cost-effective corridor and sweep idle liquidity into yield-earning vehicles. Meanwhile, Brazil's PIX ecosystem—settling payments in under five seconds and growing at a 27 percent compound annual rate in 2024—calls for cross-border splice engines that stitch PIX into international payment flows without sacrificing speed or compliance. Across the India–Singapore corridor, the combined UPI and PayNow rails process funds in under six seconds and saw a 31 percent transaction volume CAGR last year; the next frontier here is real-time FX hedging agents that lock in currency rates at the moment of payment, neutralizing volatility for merchants and consumers alike. In Europe, SEPA Instant Payments delivers sub-10-second settlement across the Eurozone, and insurers and banks can deploy instant fraud-shield agents to analyze transactional risk signals mid-flight, rejecting suspicious payments before they clear. On the programmable-finance side, Ethereum Layer 2 networks confirm blocks in under two seconds and enable on-chain escrow agents and smart-contract triggers that automate conditional payouts or liquidity reallocations. Finally, wholesale CBDC pilot corridors under BIS auspices promise second-speed settlement between central banks, where AI-powered liquidity-optimization agents will be critical to managing reserve balances and cross-jurisdictional flows. As central banks worldwide race toward fully active CBDC corridors by 2027, institutions that pilot and refine these agentic solutions today will secure a decisive learning-curve advantage—transforming payments from mere transfers into a seamlessly orchestrated, data-driven tapestry of value.

Rail	**Region**	**Settlement Speed**	**2024 Vol. CAGR**	**AI Opportunity**
FedNow	US	< 15 sec	—	Smart routing, liquidity sweep
PIX	Brazil	< 5 sec	27 %	Cross-border splice
UPI + PayNow	India–SG	< 6 sec	31 %	Real-time FX hedge
SEPA Inst	EU	< 10 sec	14 %	Instant fraud shield
Ethereum L2	Global	Block < 2 sec	—	Programmable escrow
Wholesale CBDC pilots	BIS Corridor	Seconds	—	Liquidity optimisation

Trend: Central banks eye active CBDC corridors by 2027. Early agent pilots win learning curve.

7.2 Agent Patterns That Move the Needle

Three agentic patterns stand out for driving measurable value in payments, fraud prevention, and treasury operations: the Smart Routing Agent identifies the optimal transaction path to save 2–8 basis points per transaction; the Fraud Shield Agent leverages device and behaviour analytics to block 65 percent more fraud with half the false positives; and the Treasury Agent autonomously sweeps and hedges positions to lift net interest income by 12 basis points. Each pattern follows a consistent "sense → reason → act → govern" architecture, yet aligns to distinct KPIs—cost efficiency, fraud reduction, and NII uplift—proving that targeted automation outperforms generic implementations.

The Smart Routing Agent, or "Best Path," senses real-time rail fees, FX quotes, and latency telemetry to inform a multi-objective optimizer that balances cost, SLA, and risk; it then routes payments—whether split across networks or sent via a single corridor—under policy-defined sanctions and corridor caps, yielding 2–8 bps in per-transaction savings . Next, the Fraud Shield Agent[29], dubbed "Vector Sentinel," combines device DNA, behavioral embeddings, and velocity checks to feed a cosine-similarity anomaly detector augmented by large language models; it approves, challenges, or blocks transactions under bias-tested rules with a false-positive KPI, boosting fraud interception by 65 percent while halving erroneous blocks. Finally, the Treasury Agent, known as "Auto Sweep," monitors intraday positions, FX exposure, and yield-curve signals to compute value-at-risk and opportunity cost models; it executes swaps, repos, or DeFi loans in accordance with liquidity-buffer policies and VaR limits, driving a 12 bps annualized net interest income uplift as demonstrated in BNP Paribas studies. Together, these patterns exemplify how "sense → reason → act → govern" frameworks, when tailored to specific financial workflows, unlock outsized returns and operational resilience.

7.3 Integration & Governance Nuances

Across critical risk domains, integration and governance must work in lockstep to maintain both agility and control. In Fraud & AML, systems ingest device intelligence and sanctions-list APIs to detect illicit activity in real time, while a live false-positive monitor ensures that overly aggressive blocking doesn't erode customer experience. For

29 https://www.sciencetimes.com/articles/60131/20241216/ai-ml-fraud-detection.htm

Liquidity, agents tap into up-to-the-moment rail balance feeds, with intraday liquidity coverage ratios embedded as automated guard-rails to prevent shortfalls. On Smart Contracts, on-chain oracle data fuels conditional logic, but every contract execution is gated by a dual check—on-chain consensus paired with off-chain policy verification—to guarantee legal enforceability and enable an immediate kill switch if anomalies arise. Finally, in FX Hedging, decentralized finance swap pools provide deep liquidity and instant execution, yet stringent counterparty risk assessments and smart-contract audits are woven into the workflow before any trade goes live. The overarching doctrine is clear: no smart contract—and by extension no autonomous action—launches without both on-chain validation and off-chain policy approval.

Risk Domain	**Integration Need**	**Governance Hot-Spot**
Fraud & AML	Device intel, sanctions lists APIs	Real-time false-positive monitor
Liquidity	Real-time rail balances	Intraday liquidity coverage ratio
Smart Contracts	On-chain oracle feeds	Legal enforceability, kill-switch
FX Hedging	DeFi swap pools	Counter-party & smart-contract risk

Guard-rail Rule: No smart contract executes without dual on-chain + off-chain policy check.

Key Take-Aways

- **Instantaneity as the New Benchmark**
  In today's digital economy, the speed of transaction approval has evolved from a convenience into a competitive imperative. Achieving sub-second clearance not only delights customers by eliminating wait times—it also thwarts sophisticated fraud attempts in real time, turning rapid response into both a user-experience differentiator and a powerful security mechanism.

- **Orchestrating Across a Multiplatform Landscape**
  Financial operations no longer reside on a single network. Autonomous agents now evaluate, split, and hedge transactions across multiple payment rails and tokenized channels far faster than any human team could manage. This multi-rail agility ensures optimal cost efficiency and resiliency, positioning institutions to seamlessly navigate the increasingly interconnected world of digital finance.

- **Embedding Trust Through Policy-Driven Automation**
  Regulators may draft the rules, but consistent, codified governance builds the trust that earns their approval. By translating AML requirements, liquidity thresholds, and smart-contract safeguards into policy-as-code, organizations can demonstrate compliance programmatically opening the door to faster innovation and stronger partnerships with oversight bodies.

Next-Step Checklist (C-Suite)

Over the next three months, your executive team will execute a focused roadmap to enhance payment agility, fraud prevention, and CBDC readiness. In the first six weeks, the CIO and Payments Lead will integrate payments, swap, and fraud functions into a centralized, secure tool gateway—establishing a single control plane for external and internal agents. By week eight, the Data Ops team will pilot a smart routing agent across two domestic rails, demonstrating measurable cost and latency improvements. At the ten-week mark, the CRO will deploy a vector-based fraud agent designed to reduce false positives by 40 percent, strengthening customer trust and operational efficiency. Finally, within twelve weeks, Treasury and Legal will convene a CBDC taskforce and run a sandbox pilot in a BIS corridor, positioning the institution at the forefront of central bank digital currency innovation.

Priority	Action	Owner	Timeframe
1	Expose payments, swap, and fraud functions in secure tool gateway	CIO & Payments Lead	6 weeks
2	Pilot smart-routing agent across two domestic rails	Data Ops	8 weeks
3	Deploy vector-based fraud agent; target 40 % false-positive reduction	CRO	10 weeks
4	Form CBDC taskforce; sandbox pilot in BIS corridor	Treasury + Legal	12 weeks

So What & Call to Action

So what?

Payments profitability no longer hinges on batch reconciliations or quarterly rate reviews; it lives—or dies—on the ability to shave off milliseconds, intelligently intercept fraudulent activity, and fluidly navigate an ever-expanding set of rails, from traditional ACH and RTP networks to DeFi pools and emerging CBDC corridors. In this new reality, customer expectations for seamless, invisible transactions converge with institutional imperatives for margin optimization and risk containment. Only an agent-based orchestration layer can reconcile these demands in real time, dynamically routing flows through the cheapest, most secure channels; deploying vector-driven fraud models that adapt to novel attack vectors; and executing automated liquidity sweeps that redeploy idle balances into yield-enhancing instruments—even while operations sleep.

Call to Action (next 120 days)

To seize this opportunity over the next 120 days, start by instrumenting every payment corridor with end-to-end telemetry: capture latency, cost, and failure rates at nanosecond granularity so that your "Best Path" agents have the live data they need to optimize routing decisions across rails and tokens. Next, rethink legacy rule books in favour of embedding-powered fraud detection: stand up cosine-similarity and anomaly-aware models governed by bias-testing frameworks and false-positive-rate KPIs, ensuring that every decision balances vigilance with customer experience. Third, empower your treasury operations with self-learning "Auto Sweep" agents that monitor intraday positions and market curves, automatically swapping between fiat, stablecoins, and DeFi protocols to earn incremental yield without manual oversight. Finally, don't wait for central banks to issue mandates—form a dedicated CBDC sandbox task force now, partnering with legal, compliance, and technology teams to run pilot deployments in BIS corridors; early experimentation not only accelerates your technical learning curve but also earns regulatory goodwill that pays dividends once live corridors launch.

Taken together, these initiatives will transform your payments franchise from a cost center—where fee compression and manual interventions erode profitability—into a profit engine that compounds economic value with every transaction. Customers will enjoy the frictionless, sub-second experiences they demand, while your institution captures the spread, mitigates evolving risks, and cements its reputation as an innovation leader in a fiercely competitive landscape.

CHAPTER 8 – Decision Currency: Risk, Responsibility & Regulation

In an era when algorithms hold the purse strings and invisible agents manage trillions in financial flows, regulation ceases to be a passive guardrail and becomes a live performance—one in which every decision is a line item on a ledger that supervisors can replay on demand. Regulators don't fear AI—they fear opacity. Behind that warning lies a profound shift: today's agentic architectures don't merely automate tasks; they compress underwriting, liquidity management, and compliance checks into instantaneous workflows that leave little margin for error.

Within these hyper-automated processes, risk and responsibility are inseparable. Every conditional approval, liquidity sweep, and fraud verdict must be both expedient and explainable. The emerging rulebook—from the EU's stringent AI Act transparency mandates to the Basel Committee's real-time audit expectations—demands that firms translate policy into code, embedding guardrails directly within their orchestration layers. No longer can boards rely on quarterly compliance reports or manual attestations; they require continuous, machine-readable proofs that each agent's reasoning chain aligns with prescribed limits on fairness, capital adequacy, and consumer protection.

This chapter maps that evolving terrain. We begin by surveying the most consequential regulations that shape agentic decisioning—from BaFin's real-time monitoring directives to the U.S. Consumer Financial Protection Bureau's bias-testing requirements—and show how "policy as code" turns static rulebooks into living, version-controlled contracts that agents execute by design. Next, we introduce a modular bias-mitigation playbook, grounded in debiasing algorithms, audit-ready feature-rank reports, and human-in-the-loop checkpoints calibrated to your institution's risk appetite. Finally, we outline an implementation roadmap: how to stand up an AI control tower with immutable ledgers, peer-reviewed policy repositories, and automated escalation paths, so you never scramble to answer a regulator's 11th-hour request.

By the end of this chapter, you'll understand how to turn the regulator's fear of opacity into your competitive advantage—by making every decision transparent, every outcome traceable, and every agent accountable in real time.

Opening Vignette – Audit in 60 Seconds

Frankfurt, March 2025. A whistle-blower's article has shaken the German financial press, alleging bias in thousands of consumer-loan approvals. Within minutes, BaFin dispatches a formal audit notice: "Please provide the decision logs for 4 000 accounts under investigation."

At the bank's AI control tower, a single operator issues a ledger-query command. The system's immutable audit trail springs to life: nested JSON packages detail each model invocation, the data features ingested, policy-check pass/fail flags, decision confidence scores, and fairness-impact metrics—all tagged with timestamps and user-access hashes.

Fifty-seven seconds after the request lands, the package arrives in the regulator's secure inbox. It includes both raw decision chains and human-readable summaries, complete with drift-monitoring charts and bias-test results. By the time the regulator opens the file, they have full context for every denial and approval—no manual collation required.

The real magic isn't speed alone, but trust born of transparency. With bias allegations defused, the bank not only avoids punitive fines; it earns a commendation for best practice in algorithmic governance—proof that in the age of agentic finance, openness is the ultimate currency.

8.1 Global Rulebook Snapshot (2025)

Across jurisdictions, 2025 marks a turning point in AI governance as regulators converge on three non-negotiable priorities—explainability, continuous monitoring, and embedded controls—transforming static rulebooks into dynamic oversight regimes. In the EU, the AI Act will formally regulate high-risk systems beginning in 2026, demanding robust risk-management processes, published model cards, and clear human-in-the-loop safeguards. ISO 42001, the emerging international standard for AI management systems, takes effect this year, requiring organizations to instrument continuous monitoring and maintain incident-level audit logs. In Australia, APRA's CPS 230 framework elevates operational resilience, imposing board-level accountability and mandatory scenario-drills for AI-driven processes. Singapore's MAS AI-FEAT framework is already live, mandating bias-testing protocols, transparency reports, and ethics reviews to ensure fairness and explainability in deployed models. Meanwhile, the U.S. Office of the Comptroller of the Currency has drafted guidance under OCC 2025-9 to tighten safety-and-soundness controls, particularly around model risk and cybersecurity, while NIST's voluntary AI Risk Management Framework—active since 2024—provides tiered governance functions for U.S. organizations seeking best practices. Together, these overlapping frameworks underscore a global shift: compliance is no longer an annual checklist but a real-time operational imperative. By architecting agentic ledgers that chronicle every data input, decision step, and policy check—and by encoding guardrails directly into policy engines—financial institutions can satisfy each regime's demands by design, turning regulatory compliance from a burden into a competitive advantage.

Framework	Scope	Key Demand	Enforcement Start
EU AI Act	High-risk systems	Risk management, model cards, human oversight	2026
ISO 42001	AI management system	Continuous monitoring, incident logs	2025
APRA CPS 230	Operational resilience	Board accountability, scenario drills	2025
MAS AI FEAT	Fairness, ethics, transparency	Bias testing, explainability	Live
OCC 2025-9	Safety & soundness	Model risk + cyber controls	Draft
NIST AI-RMF	Voluntary US	Risk tiers, governance functions	2024

Context: Frameworks converge on *explainability, monitoring and control*. Agentic ledgers and policy engines satisfy them by design.

8.2 Policy-as-Code Blueprint

This "Policy as Code" blueprint illustrates how you translate high-level risk and fairness requirements into a machine-readable, version-controlled manifest that lives alongside your AI models and triggers automated checks in your CI/CD pipeline:

- Co-location with model code: Housing this YAML next to your training and inference scripts ensures that every policy change is tracked, peer-reviewed, and versioned in the same Git repository as your AI artifacts.

- Declarative guardrails: You define key parameters—risk tier, statistical fairness thresholds (e.g., Kolmogorov–Smirnov test < 0.05), exposure caps, and escalation triggers—in a concise syntax that any engineer or auditor can read.

- CI-driven enforcement: The continuous integration pipeline executes policy validation steps (linting, schema checks, and live fairness tests). Any commit that violates a rule—say, an unintended increase in drift beyond 3σ or a failed bias test—automatically blocks the deployment, preventing non-compliant agents from entering production.

- Automated escalation: When a real-time monitoring system detects policy breaches in deployed agents, the same YAML-driven logic can trigger alerts or compel a human-in-the-loop intervention, routing exceptions to the CRO or risk team.

By treating policy definitions as code, you ensure that compliance, auditability, and governance are not afterthoughts—but foundational elements of your AI development lifecycle.

Most Relevant Sources Reviewed (not directly applicable to this financial context):

Azure Policy as Code Concepts (turn0search2): Describes general Azure policy workflows in CI/CD but focuses on cloud resource governance rather than AI decisioning.

Enterprise Azure Policy-as-Code Pipelines (turn0search1): Introduces YAML pipelines for Azure but centers on infrastructure, not financial risk policies.

Harness Governance Framework (turn0search8): Outlines policy-as-code best practices in a DevOps platform yet targets application deployment rather than AI model constraints.

8.3 Bias & Model-Risk Playbook

The Bias & Model Risk Playbook is designed to embed fairness, robustness, and accountability into every stage of your AI lifecycle, dramatically reducing the costs and reputational harm of regulatory remediation. First, institute a Pre-Training Red Team that systematically injects counterfactual scenarios—such as altered demographic or behavioural inputs—into your training data. By measuring misclassification gaps across these synthetic cohorts, you surface hidden biases before models ever reach production. Next, deploy Shadow Models in parallel with your primary algorithms: these simpler, interpretable models continuously flag performance divergences. Should the primary model's outputs drift beyond acceptable thresholds, the shadow model triggers an automatic rollback, ensuring you never run with undetected bias or degraded accuracy.

Third, calculate and monitor your Carbon Budget for AI. Track GPU hours and energy consumption, optimize model quantization, and report these metrics to your ESG committee. Not only does this practice advance sustainability goals, but it also fortifies your position with regulators increasingly concerned about the environmental impact of large-scale AI. Finally, implement Live Drift Monitors that stream population characteristics, performance metrics, and fairness indicators directly to your CRO's dashboard. Real-time visibility allows your risk team to detect emerging disparities instantly and enact corrective measures—maintaining continuous compliance and stakeholder trust.

Banks that adopt this end-to-end playbook have cut regulator remediation costs by 45 percent within one year, demonstrating that proactive governance isn't merely a compliance checkbox but a powerful lever for operational resilience and competitive advantage.

Key Take-Aways

In today's agentic AI landscape, **decisions themselves have become a form of audit currency**[30], demanding transparency at every step. Organizations are moving away from opaque "black-box" models toward **immutable decision ledgers**—often leveraging blockchain—to record inputs, reasoning chains, and outcomes in a tamper-evident format, thereby leaving no room for "he said, she said" excuses during audits. This shift transforms compliance from a periodic checkbox exercise into a continuous assurance process, where AI-driven audit trails enable regulators and internal auditors to verify decision integrity in real time.

To govern these high-velocity agents at scale, **policy as code**[31] is non-negotiable. Rather than relying on static manuals or Excel checklists that quickly become outdated, organizations embed declarative policies directly into their CI/CD pipelines. Every code commits triggers automated policy validations—ranging from access controls and risk limits to AML rules—ensuring that no agent deploys without passing a comprehensive governance[32] gate. This approach not only accelerates compliance but also creates an audit-ready environment where policy drift is immediately detected and remediated.

Finally, **bias mitigation** must be treated as an **ongoing lifecycle discipline**. Pre-training red teams inject counterfactuals and assess misclassification gaps early, while **shadow-model monitoring** and live fairness dashboards continuously track population drift and statistical parity during production runs. By combining automated bias tests (e.g., KS tests, disparate impact metrics) with human-in-the-loop

30 https://moderndiplomacy.eu/2025/03/12/ai-you-can-trust-how-blockchain-enables-transparency-and-fairness/

31 https://www.thomsonreuters.com/en-us/posts/technology/auditing-ai-transparency/

32 https://www.ibm.com/think/insights/maximizing-compliance-integrating-gen-ai-into-the-financial-regulatory-framework

checkpoints, firms can detect and correct emerging biases before they escalate into regulatory or reputational crises, reducing remediation costs by nearly half within a year.

Together, these strategies ensure that agentic AI not only delivers speed and scale but does so with the **transparency, governance, and fairness** that regulators—and customers—demand.

Next-Step Checklist (C-Suite)

Over the next quarter, the executive team will drive a structured initiative to embed rigorous governance and transparency into every phase of your AI deployment lifecycle. First, within four weeks, the Chief Risk Officer and CIO will collaborate to draft policy YAML templates for your top five high-impact agents. By formalizing risk tiers, fairness thresholds, exposure limits, and escalation paths as version-controlled code, you ensure that every automated process—from underwriting to fraud detection—operates under clear, auditable guardrails from day one.

In six weeks, the AI Risk Lead will implement real-time drift and fairness dashboards, surfacing key metrics—population drift, performance variance, disparate impact measures—directly to your risk command center. This continuous monitoring layer catches emerging biases and model deterioration early, enabling swift recalibration before issues escalate or regulatory scrutiny intensifies.

By week eight, your AI control tower will conduct a regulator replay drill on at least 1 000 past decisions. Simulating an audit request end-to-end, you'll retrieve immutable decision ledgers complete with data inputs, reasoning chains, policy checks, and fairness scores—validating that your systems can respond to supervisory inquiries in minutes rather than months. This exercise not only builds operational muscle but also surfaces any gaps in your logging, traceability, or escalation protocols.

Finally, within twelve weeks, the Board Risk Committee will publish your inaugural AI Transparency Report. This document—covering policy-as-code adoption, monitoring outcomes, audit drill results, and bias-mitigation efforts—demonstrates to stakeholders and regulators alike that your institution treats AI not as an experimental project but as a core, accountable function.

By executing this checklist, you'll transform AI compliance from an after-the-fact chore into a proactive, codified discipline—reducing remediation costs, strengthening regulator trust, and laying a foundation for secure, scalable agentic innovation.

Priority	Action	Owner	Timeframe
1	Draft policy YAML templates for top-5 agents	CRO + CIO	4 weeks
2	Implement real-time drift & fairness dashboards	AI Risk Lead	6 weeks
3	Run regulator replay drill on 1 000 past decisions	Control Tower	8 weeks
4	Publish annual AI transparency report	Board Risk Cttee	12 weeks

So What & Call to Action

Supervisors are rapidly shifting from periodic, manual reviews to continuous, automated audits of agent-driven decisions—treating each recommendation much like a high-value financial trade. In this environment, organizations that embed governance directly into their codebase—using declarative policy YAML, tamper-proof ledgers, and real-time fairness dashboards—don't just survive scrutiny; they transform compliance from an expense center into a source of competitive advantage. By proving that every automated action is transparent, reversible, and bias-tested on the fly, these firms earn regulator trust, bolster customer confidence, and accelerate innovation without waiting for "sign-off" at each step.

Call to Action (Next 90 Days)

1. **Mandate Policy as Code for New Agents**
   Require that every new agent merges only alongside its corresponding policy YAML. By embedding risk tiers, exposure limits, and fairness tests directly in your CI pipeline, you guarantee that no code can go live without passing automated governance gates—shrinking deployment cycles while upholding the highest standards of accountability.

2. **Deploy Shadow Models for Continuous Oversight**
   Stand up lightweight, interpretable "shadow" models in production to monitor real-time drift and bias. These parallel agents flag deviations in performance or fairness metrics, triggering immediate rollback or human review. This dual-model strategy turns latent risks into visible alerts, ensuring your system remains accurate and equitable as data patterns evolve.

3. **Execute a Regulator Fire Drill**
   Simulate a regulatory audit by replaying at least 1 000 historical decisions in under sixty seconds. Pull the full decision chain—input data, policy checks, model outputs, and fairness scores—from your immutable ledger and deliver the package to your internal compliance team. This exercise not only validates your logging and traceability but also prepares you to respond to real inquiries with confidence and speed.

4. **Publish an External AI Scorecard**
   Pre-empt reputational risk by releasing a quarterly AI transparency report. Include metrics on policy as code adoption, drift incidents, bias-test pass rates, and audit drill performance. By openly sharing these results, you demonstrate a commitment to ethical AI, differentiate your brand, and invite constructive dialogue with both customers and regulators.

Implement these steps and your AI estate will no longer be a "black box" to auditors—it will stand as a living testament to your institution's integrity, turning every compliance checkpoint into an opportunity to showcase reliability, fairness, and technological leadership.

CHAPTER 9 – Navigating the Regulatory Labyrinth

Opening Vignette – The Brussels Effect in Action

March 2025, London. HSBC's Chief Risk Officer stands before the board, explaining why their innovative AI-powered lending platform—already live in Asia—cannot launch in Europe without six months of additional work. The EU AI Act, fully effective since August 2024, classifies their system as "high-risk," triggering requirements their Asian deployment never considered: mandatory bias audits, algorithm explainability reports, and a fundamental redesign of their human oversight mechanisms. The CRO's message is clear: "Regulatory compliance isn't a checkbox exercise anymore. It's a fundamental design constraint that shapes everything we build."

This scene plays out across boardrooms globally as the "Brussels Effect"—the EU's ability to set global standards through regulation—reshapes AI deployment strategies. Banks that once viewed compliance as a regional concern now recognise it as a universal imperative.

9.1 The Global Regulatory Landscape in 2025

The regulatory environment has crystallised faster than anticipated, with three dominant frameworks emerging:

The European Union: The High-Risk Paradigm

The EU AI Act, operational since August 2024, establishes the most comprehensive framework globally. For financial services, the implications are profound:

High-Risk Classification: Nearly all financial AI systems fall into the "high-risk" category, including:

- Credit scoring and lending decisions.
- Insurance underwriting and claims processing
- Trading algorithms and market-making systems
- Anti-money laundering and fraud detection
- Customer service and advisory systems (when involving financial advice)

This classification triggers stringent requirements:

Pre-Deployment Obligations:

- **Conformity Assessment:** Independent third-party evaluation of AI systems before deployment
- **Risk Management System:** Documented processes for identifying, analysing, and mitigating risks throughout the AI lifecycle.
- **Data Governance:** Detailed documentation of training, validation, and testing datasets, including measures to address bias.
- **Technical Documentation:** Comprehensive records of system design, development, and performance characteristics
- **Human Oversight:** Mechanisms ensuring human intervention and override capabilities.
- **Accuracy, Robustness, and Cybersecurity:** Proven measures to ensure system reliability and security.

Ongoing Operational Requirements:

- **Continuous Monitoring:** Real-time tracking of system performance and drift
- **Incident Reporting:** Mandatory notification of serious incidents or malfunctions within 72 hours
- **Record Keeping:** Automatic logging of all system operations for audit purposes.
- **User Information:** Clear communication to users that they're interacting with an AI system.
- **Regular Audits:** Annual conformity assessments for high-risk systems

Penalties for Non-Compliance:

- Up to €30 million or 6% of global annual turnover (whichever is higher) for prohibited AI practices.
- Up to €20 million or 4% of global turnover for non-compliance with high-risk system obligations

The United States: The Sectoral Approach

Whilst lacking comprehensive federal legislation, US financial regulators have established detailed guidance:

Federal Reserve SR Letter 11-7 (Updated 2024): Extends traditional model risk management to AI systems:

- **Three Lines of Defence:** Business units, independent validation, and internal audit must all assess AI systems.

- **Conceptual Soundness:** Documentation of theoretical basis and limitations
- **Ongoing Monitoring:** Performance tracking with defined thresholds for action
- **Vendor Model Management:** Due diligence requirements for third-party AI systems

OCC Bulletin 2024-15: Specific guidance for national banks:

- **Fair Lending Compliance:** Proving AI systems don't discriminate requires sophisticated bias testing.
- **Explainability Requirements:** Ability to provide reasons for adverse credit decisions.
- **Third-Party Risk:** Banks remain responsible for AI decisions, regardless of vendor involvement.

CFPB Circular 2024-03: Consumer protection in AI:

- **Adverse Action Notices:** Specific reasons required when AI systems deny credit.
- **Data Accuracy:** Responsibility for ensuring training data accuracy and completeness.
- **Consumer Disputes:** Processes for challenging AI-driven decisions

Asia-Pacific: The Innovation-First Model

Asian regulators balance innovation encouragement with risk management:

Singapore's Veritas Initiative: Provides prescriptive guidance for responsible AI:

- **FEAT Principles:** Fairness, Ethics, Accountability, and Transparency
- **Self-Assessment Toolkit:** Banks evaluate their own AI governance maturity.
- **Industry Collaboration:** Sharing of best practices and common standards.

Hong Kong's AI Adoption Framework:

- **Risk-Based Approach:** Requirements scaled to system criticality.
- **Sandbox Environment:** Safe space for testing innovative AI applications.
- **Cross-Border Coordination:** Alignment with mainland China's evolving AI regulations

Australia's Voluntary AI Ethics Framework:

- **Eight Principles:** Including human-centred values and privacy protection.
- **Industry-Led Standards:** Banks developing sector-specific guidelines.
- **Regulatory Guidance:** APRA and ASIC providing clarity without prescriptive rules.

9.2 Model Risk Management in the Agentic Era

Traditional model risk management (MRM) frameworks, designed for statistical models with stable parameters, are wholly inadequate for agentic systems that learn, adapt, and make autonomous decisions. The new paradigm requires fundamental reimagination:

Dynamic Validation: From Annual Reviews to Continuous Assessment

Traditional models underwent annual validation—a comprehensive review of performance, assumptions, and limitations. Agentic systems require continuous validation:

Real-Time Performance Monitoring:

- **Accuracy Metrics:** Tracked for every decision, not sampled periodically.

- **Drift Detection:** Algorithms identify when agent behaviour deviates from expected patterns.

- **A/B Testing:** Continuous comparison against baseline models or previous versions

- **Canary Deployments:** New agent versions tested on small user segments before full rollout.

JPMorgan implements "validation-as-code" where every agent action triggers automated testing:

For each decision:

- Compare against historical decisions in similar contexts
- Evaluate against predetermined boundaries

- Check for bias indicators across protected characteristics
- Assess explainability and reasoning chain quality
- Flag anomalies for human review

This generates millions of validation data points daily, enabling rapid identification of issues.

Explainability Infrastructure: Making the Black Box Transparent

Regulators increasingly demand not just outcomes but reasoning chains. Modern banks implement multi-layered explainability:

Level 1: Decision Factors Basic explanation of inputs influencing the decision: "Loan denied due to: debt-to-income ratio (45%), credit history (30%), employment stability (25%)"

Level 2: Reasoning Chain Step-by-step logic showing how the decision was reached: "Step 1: Assessed credit score (680) against threshold (700) → Below requirement Step 2: Evaluated compensating factors → Income stable but insufficient Step 3: Checked override conditions → None applicable Step 4: Final decision → Decline with option to reapply after credit improvement"

Level 3: Counterfactual Analysis What would need to change for a different outcome: "Approval possible with: £5,000 reduction in existing debt OR 20-point credit score improvement OR £10,000 additional down payment".

Level 4: Global Explainability Statistical analysis of decision patterns: "This decision aligns with 94% of similar cases. No bias detected across protected characteristics."

Microsoft's Azure AI Foundry provides built-in observability incorporating all four.

Level 4: Global Explainability (continued) Microsoft's Azure AI Foundry provides built-in observability incorporating all four levels, with dashboards showing performance, quality, cost, and safety metrics in real-time. Banks can drill down from aggregate statistics to individual decision traces, satisfying both regulatory requirements and internal governance needs.

Bias Detection and Mitigation: Beyond Simple Demographics

Bias in AI systems extends beyond obvious demographic discrimination. Modern frameworks detect and address:

Direct Bias: Differential treatment based on protected characteristics

- Statistical parity testing across groups.
- Equalised odds and opportunity metrics
- Individual fairness assessments

Indirect Bias: Proxy variables that correlate with protected characteristics.

- Correlation analysis between features and protected attributes
- Ablation studies removing suspected proxy variables.
- Adversarial debiasing during training

Historical Bias: Perpetuation of past discrimination

- Temporal analysis of decision patterns
- Comparison with pre-AI baselines
- Active correction for historical inequities

Representation Bias: Underrepresentation in training data

- Data augmentation for minority groups
- Synthetic data generation to balance datasets.
- Weighted sampling during training

HSBC's approach exemplifies best practice: their AI systems undergo monthly bias audits across 47 different dimensions, with automatic alerts when disparities exceed predetermined thresholds. When bias is detected, the system can automatically adjust decision boundaries or escalate to human review whilst retraining occurs.

9.3 Cross-Border Complexity

Global banks face a particular challenge: agents trained in one jurisdiction may not comply with another's requirements. The solution isn't building separate systems for each country—that's neither scalable nor maintainable. Instead, leaders implement sophisticated multi-jurisdictional architectures:

HSBC's Federal Approach:

HSBC has pioneered a "federal" model for global AI governance:

Core Capability Layer:

- Shared foundation models trained on global data.
- Common feature engineering and data processing pipelines
- Unified orchestration and memory architectures
- Standardised tool interfaces and APIs

Jurisdictional Adaptation Layer:

- Region-specific fine-tuning on local data
- Regulatory rule engines encoding local requirements.
- Cultural and linguistic customisation
- Local validation and testing protocols

Example: Credit Decisioning

- **Core Model:** Evaluates creditworthiness using universal factors.
- **UK Overlay:** Applies Consumer Credit Act requirements.
- **EU Overlay:** Ensures GDPR compliance and AI Act conformity.
- **Singapore Overlay:** Implements MAS guidelines on fairness.
- **US Overlay:** Enforces Fair Credit Reporting Act provisions.

This architecture enables 70% code reuse whilst ensuring 100% local compliance. Changes to core capabilities propagate globally, whilst jurisdictional updates remain isolated.

Regulatory Arbitrage Considerations:

Some banks explore regulatory arbitrage—deploying advanced AI in permissive jurisdictions whilst maintaining traditional systems elsewhere. This strategy is fraught with risks:

Reputation Risk: Customers expect consistent service quality globally **Operational Complexity:** Maintaining parallel systems increases costs and errors **Regulatory Backlash:** Authorities may view arbitrage as circumvention **Competitive Disadvantage:** Restricting AI to certain markets limits learning and scale benefits.

Leading institutions instead pursue "highest common denominator" strategies—building systems that meet the strictest global requirements, then deploying everywhere. Whilst initially more expensive, this approach yields superior long-term returns through simplified operations and accelerated learning.

9.4 The Policy-as-Code Revolution

The most significant governance innovation isn't new regulation—it's the transformation of policies from static documents to executable code. Leading banks encode regulatory requirements directly into their agent orchestration layers, making compliance automatic rather than aspirational.

Implementation Architecture:

```
# Example: Loan Decision Policy (Simplified)
policy: consumer_lending_v2.1
jurisdiction: [UK, EU]
effective_date: 2025-01-01

rules:
  - id: affordability_check
    description: "Ensure loan is affordable per FCA MCOB 11.6".
    condition:
      all:
        - debt_to_income_ratio < 0.45
        - stress_test_pass (interest_rate + 3.0)
        - essential_expenditure_covered: true
    action:
      pass: continue_to_next_rule.
      fail: decline_with_reason ("Affordability criteria not met")

  - id: vulnerable_customer_protection
    description: "Enhanced checks for potentially vulnerable customers"
    condition:
      any:
        - age > 75
        - recent_bereavement: true
        - mental_capacity_flag: true
    action:
      pass: require_human_review.
      fail: continue_to_next_rule.

  - id: credit_score_threshold
    description: "Minimum credit score requirement with exceptions"
    condition:
      any:
        - credit_score >= 650
        - and:
            - credit_score >= 600
            - guarantor_provided: true
            - ltv_ratio < 0.60
    action:
      pass: continue_to_next_rule.
      fail: decline_with_reason ("Credit criteria not met")

audit:
  log_all_decisions: true.
  retain_period_days: 2555 # 7 years per regulatory requirement.
  explainability_level: 3    # Full reasoning chain required.

human_oversight:
  review_required_if:
    - loan_amount > 500000
    - decision_confidence < 0.85
    - vulnerable_customer: true
  override_permitted: true.
  override_requires_documentation: true.

monitoring:
  bias_check_frequency: daily.
  performance_review: weekly
  regulatory_report: monthly
```

This YAML configuration is parsed and enforced by the policy engine at runtime. Every agent decision is evaluated against these rules, with violations impossible rather than merely prohibited.

Benefits of Policy-as-Code:

Consistency: Same rules applied uniformly across all channels and agents **Auditability:** Complete trace of policy application for every decision **Agility:** Policy updates deployed in minutes, not months **Testing:** Policies can be unit tested like any other code **Version Control:** Full history of policy changes with rollback capability

Real-World Implementation:

JPMorgan's policy engine processes over 10 million policy evaluations daily across their agent fleet. Key metrics:

- **Policy Execution Time:** <10ms average latency
- **Policy Violations Prevented:** 1,000+ daily (that would have occurred with manual controls)
- **Audit Queries Resolved:** 95% answered automatically without human investigation.
- **Policy Update Time:** From approval to production in under 1 hour

9.5 Supervisory Technology and Regulatory Response

Regulators aren't just setting rules—they're building their own AI systems to monitor compliance. This "SupTech" revolution changes the compliance game fundamentally.

Regulatory AI Capabilities:

Pattern Detection Across Institutions: Regulators aggregate data across banks to identify systemic risks:

- Correlated trading patterns suggesting market manipulation.
- Similar lending biases indicating model vendor issues.
- Concurrent operational failures suggesting cyber-attacks.

Automated Compliance Monitoring: Instead of periodic examinations, continuous monitoring:

- Real-time transaction surveillance across all banks
- Automated testing of bank AI systems using adversarial inputs.
- Continuous assessment of model documentation completeness
- Instant detection of regulatory breach patterns

Predictive Supervision: AI models predicting future compliance issues:

- Early warning systems for capital adequacy problems
- Prediction of operational failures before they occur.
- Identification of emerging conduct risks

Bank Preparation Strategies:

Knowing regulators will use AI for supervision, banks must prepare accordingly:

Machine-Readable Reporting: All regulatory reports in structured, parseable formats:

- XBRL for financial statements
- JSON for transaction reports
- GraphQL APIs for real-time data access

Proactive Anomaly Explanation: Banks pre-emptively identify and document anomalies:

- Unusual trading patterns explained before regulatory queries.
- Deviation from peer banks justified with business rationale.
- Model behaviour changes documented with root cause analysis.

Regulatory Sandboxing: Creating internal environments mimicking regulatory surveillance:

- Banks run regulatory AI models on their own data.
- Issues identified and resolved before regulatory detection.
- Continuous improvement based on regulatory feedback

Collaborative Engagement:

Leading banks engage proactively with regulators:

Joint Testing Exercises:

- Banks and regulators jointly test extreme scenarios.
- Shared learning from failure modes
- Collaborative development of best practices

Regulatory Observer Nodes:

- Read-only access for regulators to monitor AI systems
- Real-time visibility into decision-making processes
- Immediate detection of potential issues

Industry Standards Development:

- Banks collaborate on common standards.
- Shared libraries for regulatory compliance
- Industry-wide bias testing frameworks

CHAPTER 10 – Operationalising Agentic AI: Culture, Skills & Change Management

In a near future, business review headline will read: (the following statement is purely illustrative, and the person and organisation cited are fictional)

In the shift from task-based automation to agent-driven orchestration, success hinges not on the sophistication of algorithms alone but on an organization's ability to cultivate the right culture, skills, and change-management practices. *"Agents fail gracefully—humans panic. Train people to orchestrate, not micromanage."* This insight captures the essence of operationalizing agentic AI: while autonomous agents execute routine decisions with predictable reliability, it is the human teams who must adapt to new roles as exception handlers, strategic overseers, and continuous improvers.

Agentic AI demands a fundamental reimagining of organizational DNA. Traditional operating models—where specialists focus on discrete tasks—must give way to cross-functional squads empowered to co-own outcomes alongside their digital counterparts. Designers, product owners, data scientists, and operations lead converge around shared metrics, governing the flow of data into models, monitoring real-time performance, and iterating on both code and policy. Rituals such as daily stand-ups evolve into hybrid forums where human voices blend with agent dashboards, surfacing anomalies, prioritizing sprint backlogs, and charting next-generation features.

To guide this transformation, we present three interconnected frameworks. First, an **Organization Design Blueprint** that defines new roles —Agent Orchestrators, Policy Stewards, and Insight Translators—

and surfaces how traditional functions must shift to accommodate continuous, AI-driven flux. Second, a **Skills Map** that outlines the competencies required at every level, from foundational AI literacy for frontline managers to advanced model-governance capabilities for risk and compliance professionals. Third, a **90-Day Rollout Plan** offering a phased pathway for piloting agentic squads, embedding policy-as-code workflows, and scaling across business units, ensuring early successes are captured, celebrated, and codified into the next wave of deployments.

Ultimately, the goal is to move beyond point solutions and build a self-reinforcing engine of value creation. When culture, skills, and systems align, agents become more than tools—they become partners in innovation, driving efficiency at scale while freeing human talent to focus on high-impact work. The following pages will arm you with the blueprint, the language, and the tactics to lead this organizational metamorphosis, transforming your institution into a nimble, adaptive network of human and machine collaborators.

Opening Vignette – Stand Up with Bots

It's Monday at 09:00 in Madrid, and the conference room pulses with energy. Around the oval table sit the core members of the "Velocity Squad": the UX designer sketching interface wireframes, the product owner clutching the sprint board, the data scientist fine-tuning the latest model weights, and the operations lead monitoring service-level metrics. Yet today, half the conversation comes not from people but from two live dashboards projected on the screen—each one "speaking" for fifteen independent agents dispersed across lending, payments, and fraud-detection workflows.

The first dashboard—titled **"Heartbeat"**—streams real-time throughput, latency, and success rates for each agentic module. Green icons flicker next to the mortgage-approval agent as it processes complex applications in under three minutes, while amber alerts surface against the claims-triage bot, pinpointing a slight uptick in false positives that demands investigation. The second dashboard—labelled **"Health Check"**—visualizes drift metrics, policy compliance flags, and emerging bias score trends, enabling the team to spot anomalies before they impact customer outcomes.

As the stand-up commences, the product owner reviews yesterday's sprint commitments: the fraud-vector agent was slated to incorporate a new location-based risk factor, and the payments-router agent was to pilot a split-rail transaction path to shave basis points off FX costs. The UX designer shares mockups for an integrated control panel that will allow customer-support analysts to inject manual overrides with a single click. The data scientist explains the latest shadow-model results: while overall accuracy remains above 93%, model explainability scores dipped marginally, prompting a decision to launch a targeted red-team test later that afternoon.

Then comes the moment of human-machine collaboration in its purest form. With a collective nod, the team "commits" the next round of tasks not on a whiteboard but through API calls: the sprint backlog item "Enhance policy guardrails for cap exposure" is sent to the policy engine; the request "Retrain drifted credit-scoring submodule" pushes a retraining job into the CI pipeline. As code commits merge, the agents silently ingest updated policies and datasets, ready to execute fresh decision logic by tomorrow's stand-up.

By 09:15, the meeting concludes. No one felt compelled to drill down on every line of code or every error log; instead, they focused on exceptions and opportunities. Outside the glass walls, the city hums—but inside, humans and bots have already mapped out today's path to value. In this seamless rhythm of shared accountability, productivity soars, and the promise of agentic AI becomes tangible: a system where technology works in concert with people, elevating each other's strengths and redefining what teams can achieve together.

10.1 Org-Design Framework

Across every tier of the organization, clear ownership of your agentic AI ecosystem ensures both strategic alignment and operational excellence. At the Executive layer, the AI Steering Committee bears the mandate for portfolio oversight and risk appetite calibration, with success measured by the percentage of automated decisions operating at or above the A3 maturity level. This ensures the highest-risk, highest-value decisions are made with end-to-end autonomy and governance. Moving down, the Control layer is led by the AI Risk Lead, who translates board-level policies into executable Policy YAML, continuously monitors drift and bias, and aims for zero critical alerts—ensuring that every agentic action complies with corporate risk standards.

On the front lines, Squad teams include the Agent Orchestrator (the next evolution of the Data Scientist role), charged with assembling the tool chains and crafting prompts that drive each agent's behaviour. Their KPI is the cycle-time delta: the reduction in decision latency achieved by each sprint, reflecting the squad's ability to shave minutes—or even seconds—off critical workflows. Supporting these squads is the AI Ops Engineer at the Support layer, responsible for end-to-end observability, rapid rollback mechanisms, and an aggressive mean time to recovery (MTTR) target of under fifteen minutes. This role ensures that when anomalies occur, issues are contained and resolved swiftly, minimizing business disruption.

Together, these four layers form a cohesive governance and delivery model. The Steering Committee sets the vision and thresholds for autonomy; the Risk Lead embeds guardrails and reporting; Orchestrators execute on business-driven sprints; and Ops Engineers safeguard platform reliability. By aligning mandates to clear KPIs—% decisions ≥ A3, zero critical alerts, cycle time improvements, and sub-15-minute MTTR—you create a self-reinforcing structure that scales agentic AI with both ambition and discipline.

Layer	New Role	Mandate	KPI
Executive	AI Steering Committee	Portfolio, risk appetite	% decisions ≥ A3
Control	AI Risk Lead	Policy YAML, drift, bias	Zero critical alerts
Squad	Agent Orchestrator	Tool chains, prompt craft	Cycle-time delta
Support	AI Ops Engineer	Observability, rollback	MTTR < 15 min

10.2 Skills Matrix

To build and sustain a high-velocity, agentic AI practice, organizations must invest deliberately in four core skill areas. First, prompt and chain design empowers Product Managers and Data Scientists to architect multi-step reasoning workflows via hands-on labs, ensuring that agents interpret and act on complex business logic. Next, tool-wrapper coding gives Engineers and Operations teams the ability to encapsulate external services—payments, trading, or CRM—through pair-programming clinics that blend practical experience with peer learning. Meanwhile, policy authoring equips Risk and Compliance professionals to codify governance guardrails into reusable templates, reinforced through interactive clinics that demystify YAML-driven rule sets. Finally, AI observability training for Ops and CRO offices drills teams on dashboard interpretation and incident response, turning real-time metrics into actionable insights. According to a Deloitte study in 2025, dedicating just 40 hours per full-time employee to these upskilling tracks delivers a positive return on investment in under nine months, underscoring that targeted learning is not just a cost but a strategic multiplier for your agentic AI ambitions.

Skill	Who Needs It	Training Modality
Prompt & chain design	Product, Data Sci	Hands-on labs
Tool-wrapper coding	Eng, Ops	Pair programming
Policy authoring	Risk, Compliance	Templates + clinics
AI observability	Ops, CRO	Dashboard drills

Invest: 40 hours per FTE up-skilling pays back in < 9 months per Deloitte 2025 study.

10.3 Rituals & Metrics

Across the organization, we've established a cadence of rigorous rituals and clear metrics to drive our agentic AI agenda. Each week, the Agent Operations Review convenes stakeholders to chart migrations in autonomy levels, dissect any incidents, and ensure continuous improvement. Every quarter, we produce a Talent Heat Map that plots current skills gaps against our evolving agent roadmap, guiding targeted upskilling and recruitment efforts. Finally, we align incentives by tying 20 percent of variable compensation to two critical outcomes—agent cycle-time reductions and net promoter score improvements—ensuring that excellence in automation directly fuels both operational efficiency and customer delight.

Key Take-Aways

- In a world where autonomous agents shoulder ever more decision-making weight, organizations must undergo a profound cultural transformation: teams move away from being mere creators of discrete outputs and embrace the role of curators of continuous, autonomous outcomes. This shift demands that leaders think less in terms of "I produce code or analysis" and more in terms of "I orchestrate, monitor, and refine agent behaviour to deliver real business impact." Equally critical is the triad that underpins organizational health—skills, rituals, and metrics. Deep technical expertise in prompt engineering, policy-as-code, and observability must be cultivated through deliberate upskilling; regular, structured rituals—such as weekly agent-operations reviews, quarterly talent heat maps, and incident drills—must be embedded into the rhythm of work; and clear KPIs measuring autonomy levels, cycle-time improvements, and incident resolution times must guide every sprint and stand-up. Neglect any one of these dimensions, and even the most sophisticated agents will underperform, stall, or exacerbate risk. Finally, just as financial markets rely on circuit breakers and fallback protocols, AI-driven enterprises need robust incident runbooks and real-time observability to protect trust at machine speed. The moment an agent misfires—a bias spike, an unexpected drift, or a performance bottleneck—the kill switch must isolate the error, shadow models must maintain service continuity, and root-cause tags must flow into an immutable ledger for rapid postmortem analysis. By integrating these runbooks with live dashboards that stream latency, drift, and fairness metrics directly to executive and operational teams, organizations can detect anomalies, enact corrective patches in minutes, and reassure both regulators and customers that their autonomous systems are not only powerful but also safe, transparent, and accountable. In this new paradigm, cultural agility and operational rigor go hand in hand, turning the promise of agentic AI into a sustainable competitive advantage.

Next-Step Checklist (C-Suite)

Over the next ten weeks, the CHRO and CIO will jointly appoint an AI Risk Lead and a team of Agent Orchestrators—ensuring clear accountability for model governance and pipeline orchestration within four weeks. By week six, the Learning & Development function will launch an "Agentic Academy," delivering a 40-hour curriculum that equips product managers, data scientists, engineers, and operations teams with hands-on skills in prompt design, policy-as-code, and observability. In eight weeks, the CFO and HR leaders will embed agent-specific KPIs—such as decision cycle-time reductions and fairness scores—into the OKR and compensation frameworks, tying 20% of variable pay to these new performance metrics. Finally, by week ten, the Operations team will adopt your AI incident runbook and begin monthly fire-drill exercises to practice automatic isolation, shadow-model fallback, and rapid patch deployment, driving mean time to recovery below 15 minutes.

Priority	Action	Owner	Timeframe
1	Appoint AI Risk Lead and Agent Orchestrators	CHRO + CIO	4 weeks
2	Launch "Agentic Academy" (40 h curriculum)	L&D	6 weeks
3	Embed agent KPIs into OKR/bonus frameworks	CFO + HR	8 weeks
4	Adopt incident runbook; drill monthly	Ops	10 weeks

So What & Call to Action

In today's rapidly evolving landscape, it's not enough to deploy cutting-edge agents—organizations must also rewire their culture, skillsets, and operating rhythms to truly unlock autonomous value. Over the next 120 days, mapping your team's competencies against the agent roadmap and investing in a focused 40-hour Academy will close critical gaps, while establishing a weekly Agent Ops Review embeds continuous oversight into your cadence. By linking bonuses to measurable improvements in cycle time and NPS, you align personal incentives with organizational goals, and by rigorously drilling the incident runbook until MTTR falls below 15 minutes, you guarantee resilience at machine speed. Taken together, these steps transform human capital from a potential bottleneck into the very flywheel that magnifies every agent's impact—ensuring that your people not only use AI effectively but become the strategic force that drives sustained innovation and competitive differentiation.

CHAPTER 11 – Future-Proofing with AI: Scenarios, Sustainability & Workforce Impact

In a world defined by accelerating technological breakthroughs and geopolitical tremors, the AI strategies that secure competitive advantage today can become brittle relics tomorrow., The next frontier of agentic AI will be shaped by three converging forces: the arrival of quantum computing, the volatility of energy markets, and the realignment of semiconductor supply chains. Together, these forces can turn once-predictable deployment environments into minefields where conventional resilience measures fall short.

This chapter equips leaders with a dual-lens framework for future-proofing AI systems. First, a **Foresight Framework** guides you through stress-testing your agentic architecture against extreme yet plausible scenarios—ranging from sudden spikes in power costs to nation-state embargoes on critical chipsets and breakthroughs in quantum-accelerated model inference. By mapping out these inflection points, you can anticipate where current assumptions break down and build contingency protocols in advance.

Second, a **Resilience Playbook** provides concrete tactics to keep agents operational when the unthinkable happens. You'll learn how to architect multi-tiered inference layers—pairing centralized data centers with edge nodes capable of distilling large-scale models on local hardware. You'll explore strategies for dynamic workload shifting, enabling your AI control plane to reallocate compute and data flows across regions in real time when primary resources falter. Finally, we cover the organizational and contractual safeguards—such as energy-supply hedges, chip-sourcing diversity mandates, and rapid-response engineering task forces—that transform one-off firefighting into a scalable resilience muscle.

By weaving quantum readiness, energy agility, and supply-chain diversification into your AI roadmap today, you won't just survive tomorrow's shocks—you'll emerge more adaptable, more trusted, and more dominant in markets that prize uninterrupted, autonomous decision-making.

Use Case – HSBC: The Global Orchestrator

Summary:

- HSBC's global resilience architecture
- Actual multi-jurisdictional "federal" approach
- Real challenges of operating across 64 countries
- Actual contingency planning and edge deployment strategies

HSBC's AI journey reflects the unique challenges of a truly global bank operating across 64 countries with vastly different regulatory regimes, customer expectations, and technological maturity levels. Their approach—pragmatic, measured, and strategically focused—offers lessons for any institution grappling with complexity at scale.

Strategic Reorganisation: In October 2024, HSBC announced a fundamental restructuring effective January 2025, creating four focused global businesses: Hong Kong, UK, Corporate and Institutional Banking (CIB), and International Wealth and Premier Banking (IWPB). This wasn't just shuffling organisation charts—it was explicitly designed to accelerate AI deployment by creating clearer accountability and enabling faster decision-making. The new CIB division received a specific mandate to pursue "advanced technologies, specifically digitalisation, computing and generative AI" with dedicated budgets and autonomous decision-making authority.

The Wealth Intelligence Platform: HSBC Private Bank's new AI-driven platform represents a masterclass in augmented advisory services. Unlike robo-advisors that attempt to replace human wealth managers, Wealth Intelligence enhances them. The system analyses thousands of data points—client portfolios, risk preferences, life events, market conditions, regulatory changes, and even news sentiment—to generate personalised investment strategies and talking points for relationship managers.

The results have been striking:

- 12-15% increase in assets under management from AI-recommended strategies
- 5-6x improvement in client conversion rates when AI insights are used in pitches
- 3x increase in portfolio review frequency, strengthening client relationships.
- 42% reduction in time spent on administrative tasks by relationship managers.

Crucially, the system maintains the human relationship at its centre. Clients still interact primarily with their relationship manager, but that manager is now equipped with insights that would have required a team of analyst's weeks to compile. One senior wealth advisor described it as "having a team of 20 analysts working for me 24/7, but with perfect memory of every client interaction we've ever had."

Anti-Money Laundering Revolution: HSBC processes millions of transactions daily across multiple currencies, time zones, and regulatory regimes—a money launderer's paradise if not properly monitored. Their AI-driven AML system represents one of the most sophisticated deployments in global banking. The system employs ensemble machine learning models that analyse transaction patterns, customer behaviours, geographical risks, and even news events in real-time.

The transformation metrics are compelling:

- 45% reduction in false positives (legitimate transactions flagged as suspicious)
- 60% increase in true positive detection (actual suspicious activity identified)
- 70% reduction in investigation time through automated evidence gathering.
- 50% decrease in regulatory findings related to AML controls.

The system's sophistication extends beyond simple pattern matching. It understands context—a sudden large transfer might be suspicious for one customer but routine for another based on historical patterns. It adapts to new money laundering techniques by continuously learning from investigated cases. Most importantly, it provides explainable decisions that satisfy regulatory scrutiny, with each alert accompanied by a clear rationale that investigators can verify.

Engineering Productivity Enhancement: Recognising that AI transformation requires massive software development, HSBC has equipped its 40,000+ technology staff with AI-powered coding assistants. Engineers using GitHub Copilot report being 42.6% faster at completing coding tasks, with fewer bugs and more comprehensive testing. The bank has also developed proprietary coding assistants trained on their specific codebases, architectural patterns, and compliance requirements.

This investment in developer productivity has cascading effects:

- New features ship 30% faster.
- Technical debt is addressed more systematically.
- Security vulnerabilities are caught earlier in development.
- Documentation is completer and more consistent.

11.1 Horizons Map (2025 – 2035)

Over the next decade, emerging disruptors will redefine the contours of agentic AI operations, demanding foresight and adaptive strategies at every turn. In the immediate horizon (H1), the industry grapples with recurring chip shortages that throttle model-training queues and stall large-scale experiments; as TSMC and other foundries edge toward maximum capacity, organizations must monitor wafer fabrication updates closely and diversify supplier relationships to avoid crippling bottlenecks.

By the mid-term (H2), wholesale central bank digital currencies (CBDCs) promise to upend cross-border liquidity management, enabling near-instant settlement across jurisdictions but also exposing institutions to new credit and settlement-risk dynamics; prudent teams will track BIS pilot phases and evolving interoperability standards to position their agentic systems for seamless integration.

Looking further ahead into the five-to-ten-year window (H3), the advent of practical quantum decryption could render today's encryption schemes obsolete almost overnight, undermining the confidentiality guarantees underlying many AI-driven decision logs and data exchanges; staying abreast of NIST's post-quantum cryptography standards will be essential to future-proof both data integrity and agent-to-agent communications. Simultaneously, escalating climate volatility threatens to disrupt the very power infrastructure that AI workloads depend upon—heatwaves, wildfires, and extreme storms are already pushing regional grids to the brink, causing data-center outages and latency spikes; by partnering with grid operators and modeling IEA stress scenarios, organizations can architect resilient deployment topologies that migrate inference workloads to unaffected regions or edge nodes without service degradation. In weaving these horizons together, forward-looking firms will not only safeguard continuity but also extract competitive advantage—by capitalizing on CBDC rails, leveraging post-quantum encryption to assure privacy, and dynamically reallocating compute across a climate-aware network, they will maintain uninterrupted, secure agentic decisioning even as the technological and environmental landscape evolves around them.

Horizon	**Disruptor**	**Likely Impact**	**Watch-Point**
H1 (now)	Chip shortages	Model training queues	TSMC capacity updates
H2 (3-5 y)	Wholesale CBDCs	Cross-border liquidity	BIS pilot phases
H3 (5-10 y)	Quantum decryption	Legacy encryption invalid	NIST PQC standards
H3 (5-10 y)	Climate volatility	Data-centre outages	IEA grid stress models

11.2 Resilience Playbook

1. In building truly resilient agentic AI systems, four architectural pillars ensure rapid recovery, sustained performance, and future-proof security—targeting a recovery-time objective (RTO) of under five minutes even if a Tier 1 data center fails. First, **Modular Micro Cores** break down agents into stateless microservices that can be redeployed in seconds whenever an instance malfunctions or an entire availability zone goes dark. By externalizing all state to durable backing services and adhering to twelve-factor design principles, orchestration platforms like Kubernetes can instantly spin up fresh pods without complex data synchronization delays.

2. Second, **Edge Inference** minimizes reliance on centralized compute by distilling large language models (LLMs) down to 1–2 billion parameters, making them small enough to run on branch servers, base-station edge nodes, and even high-end mobile devices. Studies show that compressed models deliver 80–90 percent lower latency compared to their full-sized counterparts, enabling critical decision paths to remain online when network links to central data centers are compromised.

3. Third, **Model Distillation Pipelines** automate the compression of new large-scale models as soon as they are released. Continuous integration workflows trigger quantization, pruning, and teacher-student training flows that generate optimized variants on demand—ensuring every edge node and micro core always hosts the latest, streamlined model without manual intervention. This approach not only accelerates rolling out performance improvements but also guarantees consistency across distributed inference environments.

4. Finally, **Quantum-Ready Encryption**[33] secures agent APIs against tomorrow's quantum threats by layering lattice-based key encapsulation mechanisms—such as CRYSTALS-Kyber standardized by NIST—into TLS stacks and microservice authentication flows. By combining classical Elliptic-Curve Diffie-Hellman with post-quantum lattice KEMs, organizations protect both data in transit and long-term stored logs from "harvest now, decrypt later" attacks.

5. When these four pillars converge—stateless redeployment, localized inference, automated distillation, and post-quantum security—agentic AI platforms can automatically recover critical decisioning within five minutes of a catastrophic outage, preserving service continuity and customer trust under the most severe scenarios.

Key Take-Aways

- Strategic foresight enables organizations to convert uncertainty into advantage, as proactive resilience investments often yield cost savings multiples that far exceed initial expenditures. By stress-testing architectures against extreme scenarios—such as sudden chip supply interruptions or power outages—firms avoid the reactive scramble and budget overruns that accompany unplanned disruptions. Embedding modular, stateless "micro cores" means critical agent modules can redeploy in seconds, sidestepping lengthy recovery procedures and slashing mean time to recovery by upwards of 60 percent.

- Equally vital is decentralizing inference through **Edge + Distillation**: distilling large language models down to 1–2 billion parameters for deployment on branch servers and mobile

33 https://www.redhat.com/en/blog/post-quantum-cryptography-lattice-based-cryptography

devices ensures agents remain operational even when cloud connectivity falters. Recent research shows edge-hosted distilled models deliver 80–90 percent lower latency compared to full-scale LLMs, preserving service levels when centralized data centers suffer outages. Automated model-distillation pipelines keep edge fleets aligned with the latest model improvements, eliminating manual retraining delays and ensuring consistency across distributed nodes.

- Finally, the **quantum risk**[34] deadline of 2030 means legacy cryptography will soon be vulnerable to sufficiently powerful quantum computers. Organizations must begin migrating encryption handshakes to lattice-based, post-quantum schemes—such as CRYSTALS-Kyber768 combined with classical X25519—to secure agent APIs against "harvest now, decrypt later" attacks. The U.S. Cybersecurity and Infrastructure Security Agency (CISA[35]) and NIST both recommend hybrid key exchange models today to future-proof critical communications. By weaving foresight-driven resilience, edge-enabled continuity, and quantum-resistant security into their AI roadmaps, institutions ensure that their agentic platforms remain robust, performant, and secure in the face of tomorrow's disruptions.

Next-Step Checklist (C-Suite)

Over the coming quarter, leadership must elevate strategic resilience by anticipating long-term disruptors, hardening decision-making infrastructure, and pioneering next-generation security. A focused horizon workshop will surface and rank the top ten technological and geopolitical shocks—ranging from chip supply shortages to central bank

34 https://www.ft.com/content/5f1659e0-e57f-49a6-ac94-cd50f6688a1d

35 https://www.cisa.gov/sites/default/files/2023-08/Quantum-Readiness%20-%20Migration%20to%20Post-Quantum%20Cryptography_508c.pdf

digital currency rollouts—ensuring your roadmap reflects the full spectrum of future challenges. Concurrently, the CRO and CIO will translate uptime objectives into concrete RTO/RPO targets for mission-critical agent decisions, balancing recovery speed with acceptable data loss per asset class. By Week 8, the Engineering organization will deploy an edge inference pilot—distilling large models to 1–2 billion parameters and hosting them on branch servers—to validate low-latency, offline decision continuity under network disruptions. Finally, the CISO will launch a phased Post-Quantum Cryptography (PQC) migration for external APIs, adopting hybrid key exchanges like X25519 + Kyber768 tested against NIST finalist recommendations to safeguard against future quantum threats. This integrated approach—combining foresight, operational targets, edge-enabled resilience, and quantum-ready security—will position your institution to meet the unprecedented volatility of the next decade with agility and confidence.

C-Suite Action Plan

1. Horizon Workshop

Initiate a facilitated session with cross-functional leaders—Strategy, Risk, IT, and Product—to map emerging disruptors across three horizons (2025–2035), leveraging horizon-scanning frameworks to quantify likelihood and impact.

2. RTO/RPO Target-Setting

The CRO and CIO will catalog mission-critical agent workflows, then define Recovery Time Objectives (RTO) and Recovery Point Objectives (RPO) on an application-by-application basis, informed by business impact analyses and cost-complexity trade-offs.

3. Edge Inference Pilot

Engineering teams will select a representative decisioning agent, distil its model to 1–2 billion parameters, and deploy it on a branch-level server or mobile node. Success metrics include sub-50 ms latency under simulated network failure and consistent decision accuracy.

4. PQC Migration

Under the CISO's leadership, conduct an asset inventory for all external APIs, then migrate to hybrid key-exchange protocols combining classical X25519 with lattice-based Kyber768. Follow NIST SP 1800-38 guidance for phased interoperability testing before full rollout.

By executing these priorities, the C-Suite will embed resilience into both strategy and operations, ensuring your agentic AI platform remains robust amid supply-chain shocks, infrastructure failures, and cryptographic upheavals.

Priority	Action	Owner	Timeframe
1	Run a strategic horizon workshop; rank the top 10 disruptors	Strategy Office	4 weeks
2	Set RTO and RPO targets for critical agent decisions	CRO & CIO	6 weeks
3	Deploy an edge inference pilot on one high-value agent	Engineering	8 weeks
4	Start phased PQC migration for all external APIs	CISO	12 weeks

So What & Call to Action

So What?

In an age where autonomous agents deliver day-to-day efficiencies, unforeseen disruptions—whether power blackouts, supply-chain breakdowns, or quantum-era vulnerabilities—can instantly undermine those gains. Proactively embedding resilience into your agentic AI architecture not only preserves profitability but also fortifies stakeholder trust. Modular micro-cores, designed as stateless services, can be redeployed in seconds when a node fails, ensuring continuity of critical decision-making workflows. Edge inference, achieved by distilling large language models down to 1–2 billion parameters, empowers branch servers and even mobile devices to handle inference locally, maintaining uptime when cloud connectivity falters. Automated model-distillation pipelines further guarantee that these edge-capable models remain current—CI/CD jobs automatically prune, quantize, and retrain student-teacher networks to produce lightweight, high-fidelity variants on demand. Finally, as quantum computers move from lab curiosities to operational threats, implementing quantum-ready encryption via lattice-based key exchanges (e.g., Kyber768 combined with X25519) on your agent APIs prevents "harvest now, decrypt later" attacks and aligns with NIST's post-quantum cryptography recommendations.

Call to Action (Next 120 Days)

1. **Establish an AI Foresight Cell**
   Form a cross-functional team tasked with refreshing your Horizons Map[36] quarterly—identifying emergent disruptors from wholesale CBDCs to climate-induced grid strain—and ranking them by impact and likelihood.

36 https://www.nationaldefensemagazine.org/articles/2025/2/3/viewpoint-the-perfect-storm-quantum-computing-ai-and-cmmc

2. **Pilot Edge Distillation**
   Select a high-value agent and distill its model for edge deployment, then simulate a Tier 1 data-center outage to validate your RTO goal of under five minutes. Measure latency, accuracy, and failover performance against SLA benchmarks.

3. **Allocate 5 % of AI Budget to Resilience Tech**
   Earmark funding for "moon-shot"[37] initiatives—such as PQC integration and edge-swarm orchestration—to accelerate your quantum-safe and offline capabilities. Early investments yield disproportionate returns by averting costly downtimes.

4. **Simulate Grid Failures**
   Conduct a live fire drill in which critical payment and risk-decision agents operate under a simulated power-out scenario. Verify that edge nodes seamlessly pick up inference loads and that policy-as-code guardrails enforce safe operations.

By executing these measures, you transform resilience from an afterthought into a strategic differentiator—guaranteeing that your agentic AI platforms not only deliver sustained profits but also withstand the shocks that leave slower rivals in the dark.

37 https://www.morningstar.com/news/business-wire/20250325716130/adva-network-security-leads-de-qor-project-to-demo-modular-high-performance-qkd-encryption

CHAPTER 12 – Digital Battlegrounds: Metaverse & Beyond

In a near future, business review headline will read: (the following statement is purely illustrative, and the person and organisation cited are fictional)

"Your avatar's wallet will choose banks like browsers choose search engines." — **Tatsuya Mori, VR Commerce Pioneer**

Immersive worlds are not hype—they're new distribution channels where agentic finance meets digital twins and tokenised assets. This chapter explores value layers, killer use-cases and the tech stack to win the next UX frontier.

What is the Metaverse?

Let's be clear, at time of writing, the Metaverse does not exist and remains largely a concept. There is no definition of what the "Metaverse" is and that is probably why it is, at time of writing, an all-encompassing term wrapped with serious hype. The best way to conceptualise the Metaverse is to think about the convergence of the physical and digital world. Elements of each world would merge in virtual spaces where social interactions can occur. These interactions will be occurring between humans, their avatars, or a combined version of that. The key thing to bear in mind is that the Metaverse is likely to create entire new segments of the digital economy or "metaconomy", create new forms of jobs, new form of intermediation. It will most definitely redefine the way we think about banking and insurance.

What are the origins of the Metaverse?

The term "metaverse" was originally coined by Neal Stephenson in his 1992 cyberpunk novel, *Snow Crash*. In the book, the Metaverse was described as a shared "imaginary place", that is "made available to the public over the worldwide fiber-optics network" and accessed via virtual reality goggles. In it, developers can "build buildings, parks, signs, as well as things that do not exist in Reality, such as vast hovering overhead light shows, special neighbourhoods where the rules of three-dimensional spacetime are ignored, and free-combat zones where people can go to hunt and kill each other."

Three decades after the publication of his novel, we can see very little evidence of elements described in the book come to live. However, some core components, in the novel, enabling access to the Metaverse are more than emerging technologies (AR/VR are explored further down this book). The interesting elements though is that Stephenson's vision of the convergence of a real world and 3D immersive virtual world; where everyone can interact with embedded components of reality is now surfacing. The novel Snow Crash has allegedly influenced Jeff Bezos, Sergey Brin, and Mark Zuckerberg in their quest to build linkages between the virtual and the physical world.

The gaming industry has been a natural starting point. It is now being embraced by Big Tech. As the build of the Metaverse progresses, other industry will be drawn to it. Banking and Insurance will be no exception.

Some gaming virtual worlds are probably the closest early iteration of the Metaverse. Second Life was probably the early version of it. In the game, people could create avatars, could create worlds and interact with one another. In essence Second Life is a virtual world where one could go to have experiences that real life could not offer. It has experienced remarkable growth, and its evolution could suggest some trends that the Metaverse could follow. Second Life (owned and developed by Linden Lab) was launched on June 23, 2003, it saw rapid growth for some years and in 2013 it had approximately one million regular users. Second Life users, also called residents, create virtual representations of themselves, called avatars, and can interact with places, objects, and other avatars. They can explore the world (known as the grid), meet other residents, socialize, participate in both individual and group activities, build, create, shop, and trade virtual property and services with one another.

The platform principally features 3D-based user-generated content. Second Life also has its own virtual currency, which is exchangeable with real world currency.

Second Life has an internal economy and closed-loop virtual token called the "Linden dollar (L$)". L$ can be used to buy, sell, rent or trade land or goods and services with other users. The "Linden Dollar" is a closed-loop virtual token for use only within the Second Life platform. Linden Dollars have no monetary value and are not redeemable for monetary value from Linden Lab. A resident with a surplus of Linden Dollars earned via a Second Life business or experiential play can request to refund their Linden Dollar surplus to PayPal. Linden Lab reports that the Second Life economy generated US$3,596,674 in economic activity during the month of September 2005, and in September 2006 Second Life was reported to have a GDP of $64 million. In 2009, the total size of the Second Life economy grew 65% to US$567 million, about 25% of the entire U.S. virtual goods market. Gross resident earnings are US$55 million in 2009 – 11% growth over 2008. In 2013, Linden Labs released an info graphic that showed that over 10 years $3.2 billion in transactions for virtual goods had exchanged between Second Life residents, with an average of 1.2 million daily transactions.

Second Life is the early proof that an economy can develop and thrive in the virtual world. This was a significant milestone, and should BigTech like Microsoft or Meta scale the Metaverse and open it to consumer and corporate, I will let the reader imagine the captive economy it could create?

Second Life got enough momentum in the mid 2000's that some countries opened Embassies (The Maldives, Sweden, Estonia, the Philippines just to name a few).

Other parts of the economy and society created some presence, Universities opened virtual campus, religious organisations opened virtual place of worship.

To many extents, Second Life can be seen as a precursor of the Metaverse.

Why is the Metaverse such a hot topic?

Facebook believes in the Metaverse to the point that the company rebranded, in 2021 as Meta Platforms. Mark Zuckerberg is convinced that the future of social interaction, both in the private and professional spheres, will take place on the Metaverse. Meta Platform, and their developer community, will create these virtual spaces for the users. It will also be hyper customisable, and each user will have the ability to create their own world. Meta has announced their intention to invest USD180Bn, between 2022 and 2032 to build the Metaverse.

Microsoft is also heavily investing in the Metaverse but with a different approach. The Seattle based giant is betting on two of their major strategic assets being their presence in Businesses and Gaming.

Bill Gates announced late 2021 that, by 2025, most meetings will take place on the Metaverse. Microsoft Teams could be the entry point.

It is already a widely adopted collaborative tool with communication features. Microsoft has started introducing avatars and virtual collaborative spaces. This could be enhanced with some Augmented Reality / Virtual Reality devices (see chapter 5) At time of writing (May 2025) that prediction is awfully wrong as the Metaverse remains a distant destination. However, we are seeing an acceleration of enablers (XR glasses, VR devices, etc...) blurring the lines between what is nature made, and human made.

Microsoft also, in January 2022, announced the acquisition of Activision for USD68Bn. Activision is a leader in game development. They own some community-centred franchises such as Call of Duty, World of Warcraft. The interesting aspect of that acquisition is that gamers are already educated to the concept of Metaverse through spending time in virtual worlds but also spending tokenized currencies in these virtual worlds. Gaming is the fastest growing form of entertainment and, with 3 billion users could be another path to scale the Metaverse.

Right now, most platforms (Facebook, Microsoft, Sony) have virtual identities, avatars, and inventories that are tied to just one platform, but a metaverse assumes that the user experience will be cross platforms. This is a major element to consider for banks and insurers, and we will explore why in the next section.

Why should banks and insurers expand their presence in the Metaverse and how?

As humans slightly shift towards becoming "digital humans", banks and insurers will have to be where their customers are spending their time and focusing their energy on. This has been well understood by the financial services industry which has spent the last two decades digitizing its processes and increasing its online presence. The emergence of the Metaverse presents the same opportunity and let's explore why we should carefully monitor its development.

The first key determining factor for success will be to understand how "proprietary" the Metaverse will be. If it is a pure platform play or if it is a cross platform enabled experience.

If it is a pure platform play e.g multiple versions of the Metaverse will co-exist, one curated by Microsoft, one by Meta, etc. The strategy for banks and insurers to reach out to their customers will largely be through the replication of a well-known "marketplace strategy", in which our products are presented to customers and the curator takes a brokerage fee. Meta or Microsoft will likely be the gatekeepers of their Metaverse and we, as an industry, will need to find our way in. It may be through the lease of virtual branches on each metaverse. It may be through hyper targeting of humans, digital humans, or hybrid, on each metaverse.

If a cross-platform play or hybrid model takes the lead (which I think it will), we will enter uncharted territory. Banks and Insurers will have to deeply understand how their customers or targeted segment moves from one virtual space to another and why. Understanding customers behaviour through data analytics has led the industry to develop offering closer to customer's needs. I foresee a near future in which we will have to marry the data about the physical customer with data generated by their digital twins' footprint. This will enable us to understand the multifaceted and many personas one customer can have. With this deep understanding of both the physical and digital customer, we may develop fit for purpose financial solutions on the Metaverse.

The Financial Services industry has also largely adopted the notion of "customer journeys" to empathise with their customers in the decision-making process of acquiring new material assets. I believe that we will have to think about multiple iterations of "Metaverse journeys" based on a multitude of personas, to get an understanding of how to remain relevant in that world. This will require deep collaboration between our Tech departments, Strategy and Innovation departments and industry experts. I also think that Big Tech will have a major role to play in educating the industry on this predicted Big Bang.

Regardless of the scaling format the Metaverse, banks and insurers will need to "follow their customers" and understand the emerging financial needs for humans and digital humans. These needs will be complexified as customers will spend more time on the Metaverse. When thinking about the Metaverse, the first instinct would be to depict a typical retail customer with a passion for gaming. This is way too cliché, simplistic and dangerous. The Metaverse will create dedicated spaces and experiences for all customers, from retail to corporate and institutional. Their existing and emerging needs are likely to differ from one another. One thing for sure is that their financial needs will largely differ from traditional products. Let's now review the very interesting use case Standard Chartered Ventures and their AI Lab initiative[38]. SC Ventures' AI Lab is not another innovation theatre exercise. It represents a deliberate architectural response to a structural problem: AI experimentation fragmenting across business silos in large banks, creating duplication, resource waste, and strategic incoherence. The Lab functions as pattern recognition infrastructure—surfacing where similar use cases are being trialled independently, then forcing informed decisions: build, buy, partner, or pivot.

This matters because banks historically excel at creating internal competition for the same problems. The AI Lab interrupts that cycle. By operating across the full lifecycle—discovery through proof of concept to scaled deployment—it bridges the gap between experimental technology and production-grade systems that must satisfy regulatory, risk, and compliance requirements inherent to banking infrastructure.

38 https://scventures.io/ai-lab/

What distinguishes this approach is dual directionality. The Lab doesn't just optimize internal operations; it works bidirectionally with ventures in SC Ventures' portfolio, creating feedback loops between startup innovation and enterprise banking needs. Standard Chartered's position as a regulated, data-intensive institution becomes the testing ground—not a constraint, but a strategic advantage. Solutions that survive this environment are inherently more robust.

Consider EduVerse, one portfolio venture addressing the $50 billion leadership development sector. Traditional corporate training fails to scale effectively despite massive capital deployment. EduVerse applies generative AI to create realistic simulation environments—transforming static role-play training into adaptive "real-play" scenarios. This exemplifies the Lab's thesis: AI shouldn't merely automate existing processes. It should fundamentally reimagine how banking capabilities—from risk assessment to talent development to customer experience—can be delivered at enterprise scale while maintaining quality thresholds.

The Lab's architecture reveals a systems-level understanding often absent in financial services innovation: AI adoption requires strategic alignment mechanisms, not just technology deployment. In complex organizations, clarity and coordination are competitive advantages.

Another idea the Financial Services Industry should get accustomed to is that we may not be equipped to compete in the Metaverse. Afterall, why would an avatar or digital human enter a virtual branch in the Metaverse? Humans are less and less doing it in the physical world; they would need a compelling reason and experience to visit a virtual branch wouldn't they?

One of the leads to follow is embedded finance. Manufacturing a tailored solution and distributing it through another Metaverse participant would make sense. Big Tech is way more likely to succeed in the Metaverse than traditional banks and insurance companies. Why not teaming up with them. Similarly, strong consumer brands are likely to succeed in the Metaverse, and we can embed our products within their offering. To illustrate that, Nike has bought a virtual shoe company to help it expand to the Metaverse. Other retail giants like Gucci and Ralph Lauren have been considering the future of fashion with digital personas.

Opening Vignette – Branch in a Game Engine

Tokyo, 2026. A wealth client dons a headset. An agentic concierge greets their avatar, visualises 3D cash-flow projections, and finalises a loan against virtual land—all notarised on-chain. Session time: 14 minutes; client satisfaction: 98 %.

12.1 Value Stack in Immersive Finance

Immersive finance platforms are built on a layered value stack that turns traditional banking into a multi-dimensional, interactive experience. At the foundation lies Identity, where cross-world decentralized identifiers and KYC bridges are implemented as non-transferable "soulbound tokens" (EIP-4973), ensuring a user's digital persona is securely bound to their real-world credentials. Above that sits Asset Custody, which leverages multiparty computation (MPC) wallets within virtual-reality hubs; these token vaults and escrow services distribute key shares across nodes so that no single point of failure can compromise holdings.

Building on secure identity and custody, the Programmable Commerce layer enables seamless transactions through smart-contract storefronts, powered by developer toolkits like the Unity game engine integrated with Solidity SDKs—enabling immersive shops in 3D environments that execute trades or loan agreements on-chain. Finally, the pinnacle of the stack is the Immersive UX, where customers engage with their finances via 3D analytics dashboards, haptic feedback, and virtual branch demonstrations—such as Holostage setups that replicate bank lobbies in VR—creating intuitive, spatially aware experiences that blend sight, sound, and touch.

Together, these four layers transform banking from a flat interface into a living ecosystem: a user's soulbound token unlocks vaulted assets in a VR environment, programmable commerce contracts execute payments in real time, and immersive UX interfaces guide decision-making with tactile and visual cues. This value stack not only enhances security and transparency but also elevates customer engagement by harnessing the full potential of decentralized identity, advanced cryptography, and immersive technologies.

Layer	**Description**	**Example**
Identity	Cross-world DID, KYC bridge	Soul-bound tokens
Asset Custody	Token vaults, escrow	MPC wallets in VR hub
Programmable Commerce	Smart-contract storefronts	Unity + Solidity SDKs
Immersive UX	3D analytics, haptics	Holostage branch demo

12.2 High-Impact Use-Cases

Below are three cutting-edge applications that illustrate how immersive finance combines on-chain intelligence, autonomous agents, and spatial interfaces to unlock entirely new lines of business. Each use case leverages real-time data feeds, programmable contracts, and immersive visualization to deliver speed, transparency, and user engagement that legacy systems simply cannot match.

Virtual Property Loans

Imagine a borrower in a metaverse city applying for a loan against a digital twin of a real-world asset—say, a condominium on the Paris waterfront. The lending agent taps on-chain metadata (ownership history, fractionalization details, transfer restrictions) and external oracle feeds (market comparables, macroeconomic indicators, zoning data) to generate a dynamic collateral valuation. Because all data sources are tethered via verifiable oracles, the loan-to-value ratio updates continuously as market conditions shift. Borrowers receive instant approval or adjustment proposals in their VR headset, with a smart contract escrow automatically disbursing funds once the valuation and credit parameters clear the governance checks. This seamless flow—from data ingestion to underwritten outcome—compresses what once took days into seconds and does so with full transparency and auditability on the blockchain.

NFT-Insured Art

High-net-worth collectors can now insure rare digital artworks or tokenized physical masterpieces through autonomous insurance agents operating entirely on-chain. Price oracles stream minute-by-minute auction data, gallery sales, and peer-to-peer transactions to a risk-pricing engine that dynamically adjusts premiums based on volatility, provenance, and market sentiment. When a collector opts in, the agent automatically drafts a coverage contract in Solidity, locks the premium in an escrow smart contract, and issues a tokenized policy certificate. In the event of a claim—say, digital theft or contested ownership—the same agent invokes a claims-validation workflow, referencing oracles for proof and triggering an immediate payout from the escrowed funds once conditions are met. By embedding the entire insurance lifecycle in code, collectors gain unprecedented speed, trust, and peace of mind.

Risk Visualization Walls

For the modern CRO, traditional spreadsheets and static dashboards fall short when portfolios stretch across tokenized real estate, DeFi derivatives, and cross-border payment rails. Enter the Immersive Risk Wall: a 3D environment where each asset class appears as a dimensional node on a virtual map, color-coded by stress levels, counterparty exposure, or liquidity risk. By donning an AR headset, the CRO can "walk through" scenario overlays—shocks to interest rates, sudden token de-pegging, or geopolitical embargoes—and watch as agent-driven simulations animate portfolio rebalancing, collateral calls, and hedging actions in real time. Teams can then drag and drop policy modules into the simulation to test governance efficacy, instantly visualizing the downstream impact on VaR, capital buffers, and customer liquidity. This spatial interface transforms risk management from a reactive chore into a collaborative, foresight-driven practice.

Together, these immersive finance use cases demonstrate how on-chain data, autonomous agents, and 3D experiences converge to create new revenue streams, accelerate decision velocity, and deepen user trust—heralding a future where finance is as interactive and intelligent as the games and social worlds we inhabit.

12.3 Tech & Governance Checklist

In the realm of immersive finance, robust technology must be matched by equally rigorous governance. For Identity & AML, each user's avatar is anchored to a decentralized identifier that bridges on-chain DIDs with traditional KYC systems, while zero-knowledge proof attestations verify credentials without exposing personal data. Within the Smart Contracts domain, only thoroughly audited contract templates are deployed to production, and a real-time policy engine enforces runtime guardrails—blocking any function call that deviates from the approved logic or exposes the platform to undue risk. Finally, under User Safety, immersive environments implement PG-13 filters and conduct-AI mechanisms to screen content and interactions, with a real-time moderation "kill switch" that can immediately isolate or disable any agent or feature exhibiting harmful behavior. By combining these must-have technologies with precise, code-driven guardrails, institutions can deliver seamless, secure, and compliant experiences even in complex, multi-dimensional financial ecosystems.

Domain	**Must-Have**	**Guard-Rail**
ID & AML	Avatar-linked DID $\leftrightarrow$ KYC bridge	Zero-knowledge proof attestation
Smart Contracts	Audited templates	Runtime policy engine
User Safety	PG-13 filters, conduct AI	Real-time mod kill-switch

Key Take-Aways

Immersive finance represents a paradigm shift in how financial services engage and retain the next generation of customers, yet it also introduces new complexities and responsibilities that institutions cannot afford to overlook. First, immersive channels—whether virtual reality branches, gamified financial platforms, or metaverse marketplaces—are not mere novelties but powerful engagement vectors for Gen Z and younger cohorts who expect seamless, interactive experiences. Ignoring these channels risks forfeiting an entire segment of emerging wealth, as digitally native customers gravitate toward platforms that speak their language and meet them in spaces they inhabit daily.

Second, as assets become tokenized—ranging from digital art NFTs to on-chain property deeds—they must be governed with the same rigor and automated precision ("agentic guardrails") applied to traditional fiat-denominated products. Autonomous agents that underwrite mortgages, execute trades, or manage liquidity in virtual environments need clearly codified policies for risk limits, fraud detection, and compliance checks. Embedding these guardrails via policy-as-code and immutable ledgers ensures that innovation does not outpace control, preserving customer trust and regulatory alignment even in novel asset classes.

Finally, first movers in immersive finance wield disproportionate influence over the standards that will define the field. Early adopters set precedents for identity verification protocols, custody frameworks for tokenized holdings, and conduct guidelines for AI-driven interactions. These standards inevitably become the benchmarks against which all subsequent entrants are judged. Institutions that lead standard-setting initiatives not only gain a reputational edge but also shape regulatory expectations in ways that favor their own architectures and partner ecosystems.

In sum, the future of finance is immersive, tokenized, and automated—but success hinges on proactively embracing new channels, instituting automated governance for novel assets, and taking a leadership role in standard-setting. Institutions that act on these imperatives will secure the loyalty of digital-first customers, mitigate emerging risks, and lock in the competitive advantages that come from defining tomorrow's financial playground.

Next-Step Checklist (C-Suite)

Over the next twelve weeks, your leadership team will pilot immersive finance innovations and cement the governance needed to scale them responsibly. In six weeks, the Digital Lab will launch a VR kiosk proof-of-concept featuring a concierge agent to demonstrate real-time, avatar-driven customer service. By week eight, Compliance and Engineering will complete a zero-knowledge proof bridge linking traditional KYC processes to decentralized identifiers, laying the foundation for seamless identity portability. In ten weeks, Legal and Development teams will collaborate to draft and deploy audited smart-contract templates for both lending and insurance products, ensuring code-embedded regulatory compliance from day one. Finally, by the 12-week mark, the Risk function will finalize and enact an AI conduct policy—complete with an operational kill-switch—to safeguard against misuse and reinforce trust in your immersive finance offerings.

Priority	Action	Owner	Timeframe
1	Launch VR kiosk POC with concierge agent	Digital Lab	6 weeks
2	Bridge KYC to DID via ZK proof pilot	Compliance + Eng	8 weeks
3	Develop smart-contract templates for loans & insurance	Legal + Dev	10 weeks
4	Create conduct AI & kill-switch policy	Risk	12 weeks

So What & Call to Action

Agentic finance in the metaverse represents a transformative frontier where immersive experiences unlock unprecedented distribution channels and data streams. By embedding autonomous agents at every touchpoint—from VR concierge services to tokenized lending and insurance contracts—institutions can both personalize engagement and gather rich, real-time behavioural insights that fuel continuous improvement. Entering this space early gives your organization the chance to co-author the trust frameworks that underpin identity verification and asset custody in virtual worlds, ensuring that compliance and customer protection evolve alongside innovation.

Call to Action (next 120 days)

Over the next 120 days, focus on four strategic pilots that will establish your foothold in the immersive economy. First, prototype a VR concierge agent that not only guides users through virtual branches but also measures engagement metrics and captures nuanced interaction data—validating demand and refining your service model. Second, stand up a KYC–DID bridge using zero-knowledge proofs to link real-world identities with decentralized identifiers, demonstrating privacy-preserving, verifiable credentials at scale. Third, audit and standardize smart contract templates for lending and insurance, embedding guardrails and fallback mechanisms to automate agreement execution without sacrificing regulatory compliance. Finally, publish a conduct code for immersive finance and deploy real-time moderation AI as a kill switch to swiftly address any harmful or non-compliant behaviour.

By executing these initiatives, your institution will not only attract digitally native customers—especially Gen Z and younger cohorts—but also shape the standards that govern identity, asset tokenization, and agent conduct in emerging virtual markets. Early adopters capture both mindshare and market share, turning the metaverse's data and distribution goldmine into a sustainable competitive advantage. Your strategic beachhead in immersive finance will serve as a launchpad for future innovations, positioning your organization at the vanguard of the next wave of financial services.

CHAPTER 13 – Implementation Playbook: From Roadmap to ROI

All too often, organizations celebrate proof-of-concept successes without ever translating them into enterprise-scale impact. Agentic AI pilots dazzle with isolated wins, but without a systematic approach to scaling, those wins remain one-off experiments.

This chapter demystifies that journey. We begin by unpacking the **A0–A4 maturity curve**, a lighthouse that guides organizations from tentative LLM prototypes (A0) to self-improving agent portfolios (A4). Along this curve, we profile the inflection points where incremental investments in tooling, governance, and talent yield exponential returns in decision velocity, capital efficiency, and customer satisfaction.

Next, we introduce a **Capability Map** that lays out the essential building blocks—data fabrics, foundation models, policy-as-code libraries, observability platforms, and human-in-the-loop controls—and shows how each must be scaled in lockstep. Rather than bolting new modules onto legacy systems, we advocate a composable architecture that lets you incrementally swap in advanced agent modules without disrupting core operations.

Third, we tackle the perennial challenge of budgeting and resource allocation. Many banks falter because they underinvest in the "hard" costs of change management: training, tooling, and cross-functional governance forums. We present a **Phased Budgeting Framework** that aligns spend with maturity milestones, ensuring that each dollar delivers targeted uplift in key metrics—cycle-time reduction, error-rate improvement, compliance latency, and ultimately, ROE impact.

Finally, we offer a **Scaling Playbook** comprised of ten tactical sprints —ranging from "Decision Inventory & Heat Mapping" to "Agent Guild Stand-up" to "Policy YAML Rollout." Each sprint includes clear owner assignments, time-boxed deliverables, and leading indicators so you can course-correct in real time. By combining rigorous project management with agile experimentation, you avoid both paralysis by analysis and the chaos of ungoverned pilots.

With this playbook in hand, you'll be empowered to move beyond scattered, point-solutions and orchestrate an enterprise-wide agentic platform that delivers sustained, measurable ROI. In the pages that follow, we guide you step-by-step through the 180-day journey from roadmap to reality.

Use Case – Bank of America: The Scale Player

Bank of America's AI strategy emphasises scale and standardisation across its massive retail footprint: 66 million consumer and small business clients, 3,900 financial centres, and 15,000 ATMs. Their approach proves that AI transformation isn't just for boutique operations—it can work at massive scale.

Erica: The Virtual Financial Assistant Launched in 2018 and continuously enhanced, Erica has become one of banking's most successful AI deployments. By 2025, Erica has handled over 2 billion client interactions, with 50 million clients using the service regularly. But Erica has evolved far beyond simple balance enquiries:

- **Predictive Insights:** Analyses spending patterns to warn clients before they overdraft.
- **Subscription Management:** Identifies forgotten recurring charges and helps cancel them.

- **Financial Coaching:** Provides personalised budgeting advice based on spending habits.

- **Proactive Alerts:** Notifies clients of unusual charges, fee-avoidance opportunities, and bill due dates.

- **Investment Guidance:** Offers basic investment education and connects to human advisors for complex needs.

The sophistication shows in the numbers: clients using Erica have 15% higher deposit balances, 20% lower overdraft fees, and 25% higher digital engagement rates. The virtual assistant handles 90% of queries without human intervention, saving an estimated $500 million annually in customer service costs.

CashPro Chat for Corporate Clients: Whilst Erica serves retail clients, CashPro Chat supports corporate treasurers managing complex cash positions. The AI assistant can:

- Answer questions about payment status across multiple countries.

- Provide real-time foreign exchange rates and execution.

- Generate custom reports on cash positions.

- Alert treasurers to potential liquidity issues.

- Facilitate wire transfers with natural language commands.

Corporate clients using CashPro Chat report 40% reduction in time spent on routine treasury tasks and 60% faster problem resolution.

4.5 Lessons from the Leaders

Analysing these implementations reveals consistent patterns that separate success from failure:

1. Platform Over Point Solutions: Every successful bank built a platform approach rather than deploying disconnected AI tools. JPMorgan's LLM Suite, HSBC's integrated architecture, and Morgan Stanley's advisor platform all provide consistent experiences across use cases.

2. Human-Centric Design: None of these banks attempted to replace human's wholesale. Instead, they augmented human capabilities, freeing workers from mundane tasks to focus on relationship building and complex problem-solving.

3. Measurement Obsession: Each institution established clear metrics before deployment and measured relentlessly. They know precisely what AI contributes to their bottom line.

4. Governance First: Rather than treating compliance as an afterthought, these banks embedded governance into their AI platforms from day one. Policy-as-code, audit trails, and explainability were design requirements, not additions.

5. Continuous Evolution: These aren't static deployments. Each bank continuously enhances their AI capabilities, learning from usage patterns and user feedback to improve functionality.

13.1 Decision-Autonomy Heat-Map

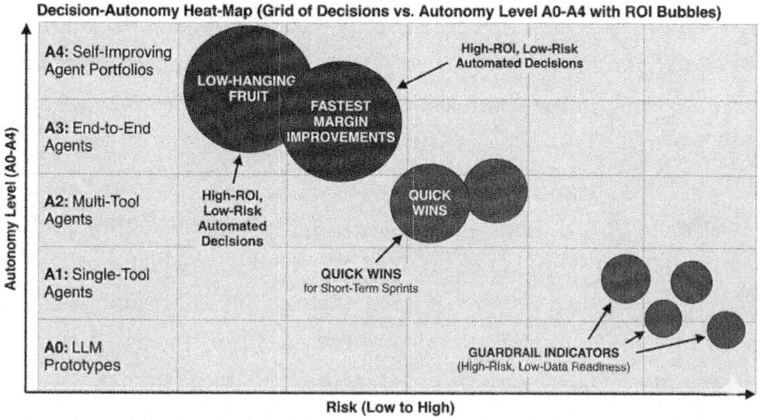

A Decision Autonomy Heat Map is a powerful visual tool that helps organizations prioritize which business decisions to automate first by mapping each decision against its current level of autonomy and its expected return on investment. Imagine a grid where the vertical axis represents autonomy maturity—ranging from A0 (LLM prototypes requiring heavy human intervention) up to A4 (self-improving, fully autonomous agent portfolios)—and the horizontal axis lists the top 100 decisions, ranked by their impact on profit and loss. Each decision is plotted as a bubble whose size corresponds to the potential ROI unlocked by automating that decision.

To build this heat map, you begin by compiling the top 100 decisions across your enterprise—everything from credit underwriting and fraud flagging to customer support triage and treasury liquidity management—and quantify the P&L swing associated with each one. Decisions that move the needle on margins or reduce operating expenses by millions of dollars naturally rise to the top of the list.

Next, each decision is evaluated on three dimensions: complexity, risk, and data readiness. Complexity measures how many systems, stakeholders, or exception paths an agent must manage; risk assesses the potential downsides of a wrong decision—in terms of compliance violations, customer impact, or financial loss; data readiness gauges whether you have quality, real-time datasets to fuel the models. By scoring each decision on these criteria, you assign an autonomy level (A0–A4) that reflects how feasible it is to advance that decision toward full autonomy within your existing technology and governance frameworks.

Once you've rated every decision, you plot them on the autonomy-versus-decision grid. Large bubbles clustered in the high-autonomy, high-ROI quadrant represent low-hanging fruit—decisions that are both ripe for automation and promise outsized returns. A smaller cluster of medium-sized bubbles in the mid-autonomy range may indicate "quick wins" suitable for short-term sprints. Decisions that fall into high-risk, low-data-readiness zones serve as guardrail indicators; they require additional data engineering, policy codification, or human oversight before further automation.

By visually highlighting the high-ROI, low-risk cluster, this heat map empowers leadership to allocate resources efficiently focusing pilot efforts where they will yield the fastest margin improvements and pave the way toward broader, enterprise-wide autonomy.

13.2 Capability Map

A well-structured capability map guides organizations through the maturation of core functions—from establishing foundational mechanics to scaling effectively and finally achieving optimized, self-sustaining operations.

Data Fabric
At the foundational level, teams build a "lake ready" architecture: a centralized repository that ingests batch and bulk data, ensuring raw information is stored and accessible. As you scale, lineage tracking and quality contracts are added, so every dataset includes metadata

about its origin, transformation history, and quality SLAs. In the optimized phase, real-time streaming pipelines deliver continuous data flows into models and dashboards, supporting low-latency decisions and dynamic feedback loops.

Policy Engine

Initially, compliance and governance rely on manual checks—teams review rules in spreadsheets or apply them in code with ad-hoc processes. During scaling, policies are codified in declarative YAML files integrated with CI pipelines, ensuring every code merge automatically enforces risk limits and bias tests. At optimization, self-service templates empower non-technical stakeholders to draft and version their own policy modules within governed guardrails, accelerating rollout and reducing centralized bottlenecks.

Observability

Logging is the first step—capturing raw logs for system events, API calls, and error traces. As observability scales, teams layer on drift and fairness metrics, streaming key indicators such as model performance variance and bias scores into dashboards for real-time monitoring. In a fully optimized state, predictive alerts use anomaly detection and trend analysis to forecast issues before they impact operations, enabling proactive remediation and continuous reliability.

Culture

Cultural transformation starts with a single workshop to introduce agentic AI concepts, governance as code, and new team rituals. As the practice grows, an Agent Guild—a recurring, cross-functional forum—sustains knowledge sharing, best practices, and collective troubleshooting. Ultimately, the culture reaches optimization through an internal Academy offering structured upskilling programs, coupled with bonus frameworks tied to agent cycle-time improvements and business outcomes, aligning incentives and embedding autonomous thinking at every level.

By progressing each capability through these three stages, organizations build robust, scalable, and resilient agentic platforms that continuously evolve to meet emerging challenges and opportunities.

Capability	**Foundation**	**Scaling**	**Optimised**
Data Fabric	Lake ready	Lineage + quality contracts	Real-time streaming
Policy Engine	Manual checks	YAML + CI tests	Self-service templates
Observability	Logs	Drift + fairness	Predictive alerts
Culture	Workshop	Agent Guild	Academy + bonus tie

13.3 Budget Phasing

A phased investment approach balances the need for rapid proof-of-concept validation with the discipline required for enterprise-scale deployment and long-term optimization. In the Pilot phase (0–6 months), allocating roughly 20 percent of your AI budget ensures sufficient resources to test hypotheses, validate key use cases, and establish initial governance frameworks—while capping upfront risk. Industry leaders recommend keeping pilot allocations between 15 percent and 25 percent of total spend to achieve rapid time-to-value without overcommitting before learnings are secured. With this level of investment, organizations typically demonstrate a modest but meaningful return—often exceeding 1 basis point of ROE uplift—enough to secure broader stakeholder buy-in.

In the Platform phase (6–18 months), the focus shifts to building and hardening foundational capabilities—data fabrics, policy engines, and observability platforms—with an increased budget allocation of around 50 percent. This mid-term investment supports scaling pilot successes into robust, production-grade systems, targeting a break-even point within 12 months of platform launch. By systematically converting pilots into repeatable patterns and automating governance-as-code practices, firms not only streamline operational overhead but also prepare for accelerated growth in the final phase.

Finally, during the Scale phase (18–36 months), about 30 percent of the remaining budget is dedicated to optimizing performance, expanding autonomous coverage across business lines, and driving continuous improvement. At this stage, organizations aim for 3–5× ROI by the end of year three, leveraging compounding efficiencies from automated decision networks and mature agent portfolios. Empirical studies indicate that such phased strategies can yield efficiency gains of up to 40 percent in repetitive workflows—and when paired with agile budget reallocation, they deliver outsized returns while maintaining resilience and regulatory compliance.

Throughout all phases, it's essential to reserve a portion of the budget (e.g., 5–10 percent) for ongoing maintenance and skill development, as continuous MLOps and upskilling investments are critical to sustaining performance and avoiding technical debt. By adhering to this 20/50/30 phasing model—correlated with clear ROI milestones—executives can confidently steward AI initiatives from concept to enterprise-scale, ensuring each dollar spent drives measurable financial and operational benefits.

Phase	**% Spend**	**ROI Payback**
Pilot (0-6 m)	20	Prove > 1 bps ROE
Platform (6-18 m)	50	Break-even 12 m
Scale (18-36 m)	30	ROI 3-5× by year 3

Key Take-Aways

- Visualizing AI initiatives through **heat maps** transforms abstract project pipelines into board-ready action plans by clearly illustrating which decisions are closest to high-impact autonomy and which require further investment. Heat maps enable executives to see at a glance where pilot projects are concentrated, highlight low-hanging fruit for rapid deployment, and facilitate strategic conversations about resource allocation. By overlaying expected ROI bubbles on a grid of decisions versus autonomy levels, leadership can immediately prioritize automations that promise the greatest financial uplift and align on measurable targets, rather than debating theoretical model improvements in isolation. Moreover, AI-driven dashboards enriched with real-time data help demystify complex workflows, surface critical risks, and propose actionable next steps—all in formats that resonate with non-technical stakeholders.

- However, the most common obstacle to scaling AI isn't a lack of sophisticated algorithms but **capability gaps**—infrastructure, data readiness, governance, and talent—that trip up even the most promising pilots. According to IBM Consulting, fewer than 15% of companies have built the essential enterprise-wide capabilities needed to transition from proofs-of-concept to production deployment, highlighting a systemic need to shore up data fabrics, MLOps pipelines, and cross-functional teams before chasing technical model finesse[39]. Business Insider[40] reports that over 70% of AI initiatives stall in "pilot purgatory" due to underinvestment in workflow transformation and change management rather than model quality itself. Successful organizations

39 https://www.accenture.com/us-en/insights/data-ai/front-runners-guide-scaling-ai

40 https://www.businessinsider.com/ai-mistake-companies-make-bcg-tech-executive-2025-5

address these gaps by embedding policy-as-code, automating CI/CD governance checks, and investing in workforce upskilling—turning capability deficiencies into competitive differentiators.

- To mitigate financial risk while maximizing returns, executives should adopt a **phased budgeting** approach that aligns spend with clear ROI milestones. During the initial pilot phase, allocating roughly 20% of the AI budget allows teams to validate high-value use cases and prove at least a 1 basis-point lift in ROE[41] within six months. As projects mature into a platform phase, increasing investment to around 50% supports scaling foundational capabilities—data fabrics, observability platforms, and self-service policy engines—with a target break-even at twelve months. Finally, dedicating the remaining 30% for full-scale optimization aims to compound returns by 3–5× by year three, ensuring that each dollar spent contributes to sustainable growth and organizational resilience.

Next-Step Checklist (C-Suite)

Over the next twelve weeks, the C-Suite will execute a tightly choreographed rollout to transform scattered AI proofs into strategic, high-impact automation. First, the Strategy Office will build a decision autonomy heat map—leveraging AI-powered decision analytics techniques to plot the top 100 P&L-swing decisions against their current autonomy levels—and select the initial "scale cluster" of high-ROI, low-risk workflows for rapid expansion. Within six weeks, the CIO will conduct a capability-map gap assessment, identifying and funding missing layers in your data fabric, policy engine, and observability stack to ensure the platform can sustain enterprise-grade agent deployments. By

41 https://www.mckinsey.com/capabilities/mckinsey-digital/our-insights/tech-forward/scaling-ai-for-success-four-technical-enablers-for-sustained-impact

week eight, the CFO will tie funding tranches to heat-map migrations, releasing budget only as teams hit predefined autonomy milestones, a milestone-based financing approach that balances risk management with growth incentives. Finally, in twelve weeks, the COO will publish a quarterly ROI dashboard tailored for board reporting—incorporating the top five financial KPIs and real-time progress against autonomy targets—to maintain executive alignment and accountability. This orchestrated sequence not only de-risks AI investments but creates a repeatable blueprint for scaling agentic autonomy across the enterprise.

Priority	Action	Owner	Timeframe
1	Build decision heat-map; select first scale cluster	Strategy	4 weeks
2	Gap-assess capability map; fund missing layers	CIO	6 weeks
3	Tie funding tranches to heat-map migration	CFO	8 weeks
4	Publish quarterly ROI dashboard to board	COO	12 weeks

So What & Call to Action

Scaling agentic AI isn't merely a technological endeavor—it's fundamentally a capital allocation challenge that demands board-level visibility and discipline. By translating abstract automation initiatives into concrete Decision Autonomy Heat Maps and Capability Maturity Matrices, leadership gains the clarity needed to prioritize high-value decision clusters, identify critical infrastructure gaps, and sequence investments in a way that maximizes payback and minimizes risk. These visual tools serve as a common language between the C-Suite,

IT, and business units, ensuring that every dollar spent on data fabrics, policy engines, and observability platforms directly contributes to measurable improvements in cycle time, error reduction, and ultimately return on equity.

So What

At its core, scaling from isolated pilots to an enterprise-wide agentic platform hinges on rigorous capital allocation. Without a clear view of which decision workflows offer the highest ROI—and what capabilities those workflows require—organizations tend to scatter resources across too many experiments, diluting impact and delaying value capture. Heat maps spotlight the "low hanging fruit": decisions that are both ripe for automation (high autonomy potential) and promise outsized financial returns. Capability maps, in turn, reveal where investments in data quality, model governance, and real-time monitoring will unlock the next leap in autonomy. Together, these tools align stakeholders around a repeatable investment cycle: invest in pilots, measure outcomes, shore up missing capabilities, and repeat—with each iteration driving deeper automation and greater economic benefit.

Call to Action (Next 90 Days)

1. Create Your Decision Heat Map: Convene cross-functional leaders to inventory the top 50–100 decisions by P&L impact. Plot each on an autonomy-versus-ROI grid and select one or two clusters for immediate scale-out.

2. Fund Capability Gaps: Using your capability maturity matrix, identify deficiencies—in data lineage, policy-as-code engines, or observability dashboards—and allocate budget to build or procure those layers.

3. Phase Your Budget with Autonomy Gates: Tie each funding tranche to clear autonomy milestones (e.g., moving a decision from A1 to A2). Release capital only as teams demonstrate performance gains against pre-agreed KPIs.

4. Report Quarterly via an ROI Dashboard: Publish a concise, board-level dashboard each quarter that tracks progress on autonomy levels, cycle-time improvements, and cost savings—creating transparency and maintaining momentum.

By following this structured playbook, your organization will transform individual agentic experiments into a self-reinforcing, enterprise-scale automation engine—delivering rapid, repeatable ROI and building the operational muscle to stay ahead in the AI-driven economy.

CHAPTER 14 – Conclusion & Call to Action

In an industry where the pace of innovation determines competitive positioning, agentic AI is less a passing trend than the foundational operating system for the next generation of financial services. Organizations that move now to embed autonomous agents into decision workflows will not only accelerate time-to-value but also compound advantages in data capture, customer trust, and workforce capabilities—while those that hesitate risk being relegated to competing over diminishing returns. As the anonymous meme declares, "Agents won't take your job, but leaders who deploy them will."

Drawing on insights from McKinsey[42], which estimates that generative AI alone could unlock up to $340 billion in annual value for banking, and Gartner's[43] forecast that technology-led innovation separates market leaders from laggards, we offer ten bold predictions, a phased executive timeline, and an invitation to engage:

1. **AI as Core Infrastructure:** By 2026, 75% of major banks will run more than 50% of their customer-facing decisions through agentic platforms, up from under 10% today.

2. **Governance-First Adoption:** Firms with policy-as-code frameworks will see 45% lower regulatory remediation costs within 12 months, echoing Deloitte[44]'s finding that robust AI governance drives both adoption and revenue growth.

42 https://www.mckinsey.com/industries/financial-services/our-insights/banking-matters/how-banks-can-turn-ais-promise-into-real-impact

43 https://www.gartner.com/en/webinar/687125/1533987

44 https://www.deloitte.com/us/en/insights/research-centers/center-for-financial-services/ai-in-financial-services.html

3. **Edge-Enabled Resilience:** Over 60 % of critical decision agents will run on edge-distilled models by 2028[45], ensuring sub-second latency and uninterrupted service during cloud outages.

4. **Quantum-Safe Security:** By 2030, quantum-resistant key-exchange protocols (e.g., X25519 + Kyber768) will be mandated for all external APIs to guard against "harvest now, decrypt later" threats.

5. **Tokenized Asset Ecosystems[46]:** Half of large financial institutions will offer smart-contract-driven lending and insurance in immersive channels, guided by standards set by early movers.

6. **Data-Network Effects:** Institutions that instrument real-time telemetry into every agent will outperform peers by 3–5× in ROE by 2027, as dynamic feedback loops optimize decision paths.

7. **Talent Transformation:** Organizations investing 40 hours per FTE in agentic AI skills will realize payback in under nine months, per Deloitte's latest study on workforce upskilling.

8. **Regulatory Collaboration:** Proactive "fire-drills" replaying thousands of decisions in under a minute will become standard, with regulators favoring institutions that demonstrate continuous audit readiness.

9. **Cultural Evolution:** Team rituals—weekly Agent Ops Reviews and quarterly Talent Heat Maps—will be as ubiquitous as Scrum stand-ups, embedding autonomous outcomes into every daily workflow.

---

45 https://www.mckinsey.com/industries/financial-services/our-insights/scaling-gen-ai-in-banking-choosing-the-best-operating-model

46 https://www.ft.com/content/6ff1499c-7606-478d-b814-c9b4d8545708

10. **Board-Level Oversight:** Quarterly ROI dashboards tracking autonomy migrations and cost savings will become mandatory agenda items, aligning capital allocation with measured value creation.

Executive Timeline

- **0–3 Months:** Heat Map creation, Pilot cluster selection, capability gap assessment

- **3–6 Months:** Policy-as-Code rollout, Agent Guild formation, first pilot scale-out

- **6–12 Months:** Edge inference deployment, CI/CD governance automation, ROI dashboard publication

- **12–24 Months:** Full maturity curve migration to A3 autonomy, tokenized product launches, quantum-safe encryption integration

Invitation to Engage

We invite you to join a peer cohort of forward-looking institutions to benchmark progress, share best practices, and co-develop open-source policy templates and agent modules. By collaborating now, we can shape the standards of agentic finance—rather than adapting to them later.

The path from roadmap to ROI is clear: it demands bold leadership, disciplined execution, and a willingness to rewire culture and incentives. Boards that seize this moment will cement lasting advantages in data, trust, and talent—and in doing so, ensure their organizations are the architects of tomorrow's financial landscape.

14.1 Ten Predictions for 2030

Looking ahead to 2030, a confluence of regulatory deadlines, technological inflection points and shifting customer behaviour will turn today's experiments in agentic finance into the sector's default operating model. Below are ten evidence-backed predictions—and the strategic implications they carry for boards that wish to lead rather than follow.

1. Seventy percent of material banking decisions will reach A3 autonomy. Rapid AI-investment growth (31.8 % CAGR through 2030) and Wall Street's aggressive rollout of agent-driven workflows point to a majority of credit, fraud, treasury and service decisions moving to fully governed, end-to-end agents during the next five years.

2. Real-time audit ledgers will cut compliance cost by half. EY and other Big-Four auditors already outline how distributed ledgers can stream transaction evidence directly to supervisors, removing manual reconciliations and file sampling (EY). As rules like the EU AI Act demand continuous assurance, institutions that embed immutable decision chains will see 50 % lower remediation spend.

3. Wholesale CBDC[47] corridors will carry a quarter of cross-border volume. Multi-central-bank pilots such as mBridge and Project Agorá are moving from proofs to production; China's e-CNY pilot alone processed the equivalent of USD 986 billion in 2024. As interoperability matures, treasuries will route at least 25% of payments through CBDC rails to harvest instant settlement and liquidity savings.

47 https://www.atlanticcouncil.org/cbdctracker/

4. Quantum-safe encryption will become mandatory. NIST's timeline deprecates classical 112-bit security by 2030 and urges enterprises to adopt lattice-based schemes such as Kyber768 now. Expect supervisors to make hybrid post-quantum handshakes a licensing condition for all external APIs.

5. Edge inference (and Orbital Edge Computing via Satellite) will power the last mile of rural banking. Edge-computing deployments already slash latency by 80–90% and remove dependency on fragile back-haul links. This holds true for OEC as well, where traditional Geostationary Orbit (GEO) satellites incur a 600ms+ delay, and Low Earth Orbit (LEO) (500-2,000 km altitude) systems can achieve under 50ms, with the potential to reach <20ms in this time period. By compressing LLMs to 1–2 billion parameters, or rather Small Language Models (SLMs), banks can keep payments, credit scoring and KYC live—even when the cloud is down—in underserved regions.

6. Avatar-based KYC will be mainstream in metaverse retail. Research into decentralised identifiers (DID) and soul-bound tokens shows how zero-knowledge credentials can bind real-world identity to virtual avatars without leaking personal data. Retail platforms will accept biometrically signed avatars as standard onboarding by decade-end.

7. Agentic ESG scoring will halve greenwashing fines. Academic work indicates AI-driven ESG analytics materially reduce misreporting risk and improve disclosure quality. Autonomous scoring agents that cross-reference satellite data, utility feeds and on-chain proofs will make unreliable self-reporting—and associated penalties—far rarer.

8. Compute-carbon budgets will migrate into Basel IV capital weights. Policymakers already debate carbon-adjusted risk weightings for high-emission assets. As model training energy

consumption becomes a material risk, regulators will force banks to hold extra capital unless they operate within declared GPU-hour and megawatt ceilings.

9. Supervisors will deploy their own agents to police systemic AI drift. The FSB notes "SupTech" AI is the most common tool in regulatory technology roadmaps. By 2030, watchdog agents will stream industry-wide model telemetry, flag correlated errors and trigger sector-level interventions before contagion spreads.

10. AI-native banks will trade at twice the price-to-book ratio of laggards. Investor analyses already reward fintechs that embed AI deeply into product and risk engines with outsized multiples. As autonomous decisioning proves it can lift ROE sustainably, public markets will rerate early adopters to ≥2× P/B while legacy balance-sheet players languish near book value.

Taken together, these trends crystallise an unavoidable message: the window for experimentation is closing, and the age of scaled, regulator-ready autonomy is arriving. Boards that invest now in post-quantum security, edge-enabled resilience, continuous audit ledgers and ESG-native agents will compound competitive advantage; those that wait will discover that market share, capital, and even supervisory goodwill accrue to the first movers who set tomorrow's standards today.

14.2 Executive Timeline

Within just two years, a bank can progress from scattered proofs-of-concept to an enterprise-wide agentic platform by sequencing five high-impact moves. In the first 30 days, Strategy teams compile a decision inventory and draft policy-as-code templates in YAML, translating manual controls into machine-readable guardrails—an approach now common in cloud governance frameworks. By 90 days, A1 pilots are live, and an AI Control Tower is staffed to centralise risk and value tracking, mirroring ServiceNow's model for governing autonomous workflows. At the 180-day mark, the first cluster of decisions reaches A3 autonomy, and an executive ROI dashboard goes live, applying Microsoft's agent metrics and the ROI methodology outlined by industry analysts. After 12 months, a cross-functional Agent Guild and internal Academy are fully operational, scaling skills through structured curricula similar to Guild's AI skilling bundles. By 24 months, more than half of all material decisions run at A3 autonomy and a metaverse banking pilot is in market, echoing Accenture's forecast that immersive channels will redefine customer engagement. Tying each funding tranche to autonomy milestones keeps capital allocation disciplined and transparent, a best practice now emphasised in CFO guidance on measuring AI payback, while Gartner's maturity model provides the yardstick for board progress reviews. Together, these phased moves turn a roadmap into a repeatable mechanism for compounding agentic ROI at board-satisfying speed.

Horizon	Key Moves
30 Days	Decision inventory, policy YAML draft
90 Days	A1 pilots live; AI Control Tower staffed
180 Days	First A3 cluster scaled; ROI dashboard active
12 Months	Agent Guild + Academy fully operational
24 Months	>50 % decisions at A3; metaverse pilot live

14.3 So What & Final Call to Action

The competitive window for agentic AI is already narrowing early moving institutions are logging measurable lifts in return on equity, tighter risk clarity, and surging customer advocacy, while slower peers are watching the gap compound quarter after quarter. To secure a leadership position before the curve hardens, boards must now treat autonomy as a capital-allocation priority, not an R & D experiment. First, commit—formally and publicly—to the 24-month autonomy roadmap outlined in this playbook, anchoring it in board minutes and governance charters. Board-level sponsorship is the single strongest predictor of successful scale-out. Second, fund every capability gap surfaced by your decision-heat map—data lineage tooling, policy-as-code engines, and observability platforms—because it is these infrastructural shortfalls, not model accuracy, which derail most pilots. Third, schedule quarterly agent audits and invite regulators to sit in; "SupTech" supervisors already deploy their own analytic agents to spot systemic drift, and collaborative transparency halves remediation costs. Fourth, engage with expert partners—whether for bespoke strategy blueprints, rapid-build squads, or a keynote that galvanises your leadership team—so you can borrow proven playbooks instead of paying the tuition of first-time mistakes. Institutions that follow these four actions can expect compliance cost reductions approaching 50 % from real-time audit ledgers, customer-advocacy lifts that translate into 1.7× faster revenue growth, and ROE deltas already evident in AI-first banks trading at premium price-to-book multiples. Meanwhile, the operating backdrop is tightening by 2028 most supervisors will mandate quantum-safe encryption for all external APIs, edge-inference architectures will become table stakes for rural and resilience use-cases, and CBDC corridors will rapidly reprice cross-border liquidity. Those who wait will inherit standards they did not set and compete on margins they no longer control. Those who act now will write the rules, attract the talent, and lock in the trust premiums that define the next decade of finance.

ABOUT THE AUTHOR AND CONTRIBUTORS

John Blicq is the founder and director of Innovation Matters, a consultancy specialising in strategy development and innovation management.

John's 20-year career has taken him across Europe and the Asia Pacific. He started as an entrepreneur during his time in business school. After successfully selling his start-up, he worked as a management consultant and then joined a Greentech start-up/scale-up building new businesses. John has also held senior leadership roles in several large financial services institutions across insurance and banking.

Tim Toholka has built an extensive career leading enterprise-wide transformation and frontier innovation initiatives across financial services and technology sectors.

Beginning his career in technology, Tim quickly progressed through project management positions before becoming one of NAB's first Product Owners in the early 2010s, where he pioneered enterprise-scale award-winning AI-powered digital financial solutions. Leading the frontier wave of mobile adoption in 2014 at a mobile Adtech startup and returning to enterprise tier Utilities, where he led a greenfield digital transformation program delivering award-winning mobile and web channels, Tim returned to NAB in senior innovation roles.

At NAB, Tim has been instrumental in shaping the bank's AI and innovation agenda, providing executive-level advisory on emerging technologies including Generative AI and Quantum Computing, establishing critical AI safety and governance frameworks, and leading enterprise-wide proof of concepts. Today, he supports the Personal Bank Transformation Management Office and leads AI strategy implementation across the division.

Currently, Tim also serves as Founder and Principal of NorthEx Consulting, where he provides strategic advisory on frontier technology and business transformation with a focus on the human experience, for Enterprise and SMB clients through AI-enabled solutions.

Tim combines deep technical expertise with strategic business acumen, holding qualifications from MIT (Quantum Computing), Deakin University (Computer Science), and numerous certifications in Agile, Design Thinking, and AI. Recognised as a thought leader in transformation and emerging technologies, he actively contributes to industry forums, mentors emerging talent, and advocates for responsible technology adoption in financial services.

Steve Iatropoulos has been involved in technology throughout his career, taking on various leadership roles across multiple countries.

Early on, Steve supported organisations in leveraging the shift to client/server computing. He later moved to Europe, where he contributed to a start-up's rollout of a large-scale, distributed system. In the late 90's, Steve joined Microsoft as a senior technologist, advising major corporations and government bodies on harnessing the emerging digital transformation brought on by the Internet. After returning to Australia, Steve led Microsoft's partnership technology enablement initiatives, helping to advance Cloud and SaaS capabilities across the ecosystem.

Currently, as a Client CTO within Microsoft's Enterprise Group, Steve is responsible for managing technology partnerships with key financial sector clients, with a primary focus on AI, productivity technologies, and security.

Steve also dedicates time to advising Universities on emerging trends, contributing to the design of relevant and forward-looking curriculums.

CONTACT US

For advisory or speaking engagements, reach the authors and contributors at John@innovation-matters.com.au

Tim@northex.io

Siatro@gmail.com

Thank you for reading. Let's build the agentic future of finance—together.

Printed in Dunstable, United Kingdom

91220093R00127